Where JESUS Walked

William H. Stephens
Editor

Broadman Press
   Nashville

© Copyright 1981 • Broadman Press
All rights reserved.

4211-38
ISBN: 0-8054-1138-0

Dewey Decimal Classification: 225.91
Subject headings: BIBLE. N.T.—GEOGRAPHY//JESUS CHRIST

Library of Congress Catalog Card Number: 80-67422
Printed in the United States of America

CONTENTS

1. Bethlehem 12
   William H. Stephens
2. Nazareth 20
   Wayne Dehoney
3. Sepphoris: Capital of Galilee 26
   Dan G. Kent
4. The Road from Nazareth to Jerusalem 30
   Wayne Dehoney
5. John the Baptist 36
   William H. Stephens
6. The Wilderness of John's Baptizing 39
   A. Stuart Arnold
7. The Wilderness of Jesus' Temptation 44
   A. Stuart Arnold
8. Christ Tempted 48
   William H. Stephens
9. Jacob's Well 50
   C. Ray Burchette, Jr.
10. Mount Gerizim 53
    James A. Brooks
11. Capernaum 56
    Jack Finegan
12. Bethsaida 63
    C. Ray Burchette, Jr.
13. The Sea of Galilee 73
    William H. Stephens

14. Kingdom Come 79
    William H. Stephens
15. The Sudden Storms of Galilee 83
    Denis Baly
16. Jesus' Wider Ministry 86
    William H. Stephens
17. Jerusalem 95
    William H. Stephens
18. The Pool of Bethesda 118
    Elmer L. Gray
19. The Gihon Spring and the Pool of Siloam 122
    Rice A. Pierce
20. Lazarus' Tomb 131
    Joe O. Lewis
21. New Testament Jericho 135
    A. O. Collins
22. Herod's Temple 142
    William H. Stephens
23. The Upper Room 155
    Richard L. Williams
24. Gethsemane and the Mount of Olives 157
    Wayne Dehoney
25. The Judgment Hall 163
    W. Murray Severance
26. Where Is Golgotha? 168
    Joseph A. Callaway
27. Emmaus 176
    Joe O. Lewis
28. Where Did the Ascension Take Place? 182
    W. Murray Severance

Authors

A. Stuart Arnold is pastor of Citadel Baptist Church, Charleston, South Carolina. He has served as January Bible Study consultant for The Sunday School Board of the Southern Baptist Convention, in which capacity he taught in Bible conferences throughout the United States. He is the author of *ABC of Bible Lands* and *How Can I Grow As a Christian?*

Denis Baly is professor of religion at Kenyon College, Gambier, Ohio. He is coauthor of *Atlas of the Biblical World,* author of *The Geography of the Bible* and *God and History in the Old Testament,* and lived many years in Palestine.

James A. Brooks is professor of New Testament at Southwestern Baptist Theological Seminary, Fort Worth, Texas. He contributed general articles to *The Broadman Bible Commentary* and *The Text and Canon of the New Testament* and is coauthor of *Syntax of New Testament Greek.*

C. Ray Burchette, Jr. is pastor of Highland Park Baptist Church, Austin, Texas, and is a frequent contributor to Bible study materials for adults and for youth.

Joseph A. Callaway is professor of Old Testament archeology and director of graduate studies at The Southern Baptist Theological Seminary, Louisville, Kentucky. He directed excavations at Ai, Israel, is an executive officer of American Schools of Oriental Research, has contributed numerous articles in the field of biblical archeology, and was coeditor of *Biblical Backgrounds,* a textbook.

A. O. Collins is professor and head of the department of religion and philosophy at Houston Baptist University, Houston, Texas, participated in excavations at Machaerus, and is the author of many articles on biblical subjects.

Wayne Dehoney is pastor of Walnut Street Baptist Church, Louisville, Kentucky, and author of several books, including *An Evangelical's Guidebook to the Holy Land* and *Preaching to Change Lives.*

Jack Finegan is professor emeritus of New Testament history and archeology at the Pacific School of Religion and Graduate Theological Union, Berkeley, California. He is the author of many books, including *Light from the Ancient Past, The Archeology of the New Testament, Archaelogical History of the Ancient Middle East, Handbook of Biblical Chronology, Hidden Record of the Life of Jesus,* and *Encountering New Testament Manuscripts.*

Elmer L. Gray is editor of *The California Southern Baptist,* former manager of the Sunday School Department of The Sunday School Board of the Southern Baptist Convention, a former pastor, and author of *Luke for the Space Age Church.*

Dan G. Kent is associate professor of Old Testament at Southwestern Baptist Theological Seminary, Fort Worth, Texas, former professor of religion at Wayland Baptist College, Plainview, Texas, former pastor, and author of *God's New People in Action* and *Layman's Bible Book Commentary: Joshua, Judges, Ruth*.

Joe O. Lewis is professor of religion and acting academic dean at Georgetown College, Georgetown, Kentucky. He is a frequent contributor to Bible study materials for adults and is the author of *Layman's Bible Book Commentary: 1 & 2 Samuel, 1 Chronicles*.

Rice A. Pierce is editor of Adult Bible study materials at The Sunday School Board of the Southern Baptist Convention, former professor of religious education at Georgetown College, Georgetown, Kentucky, and author of *Leading Dynamic Bible Study* and *How to Enjoy Bible Study with Others*.

W. Murray Severance is audiovisuals producer, Broadman Products Department, The Sunday School Board of the Southern Baptist Convention, and is author of *Pronunciation of Bible Names* (booklet and cassette), and has designed and produced *Bible Map Transparencies* and *Bible Lands, Past and Present* (overhead cel sets).

William H. Stephens is editor of *Biblical Illustrator,* former editor of *People, Upward,* and Broadman Press, has compiled or contributed to several books and is author of *The Mantle* (paperback title, *Elijah*) and *Journey Through Bible Lands* (filmstrip and cassette).

Richard L. Williams is pastor of First Baptist Church, California City, California, and has contributed articles and curriculum materials for adults and youth.

Roman Road, between Philippi and Neapolis.

RADIO AND TELEVISION COMMISSION, SBC

Preface

Jesus came into an incredible world, with an unusual pot-boiling of philosophies and religions served up on the pacified sea-lanes, roads, and the commerce of the Roman Empire. Paul saw God's hand in the timing.

Greek was an almost universal language throughout the empire; Rome had pacified the main roads and many of the minor ones; her navy had rid the Mediterranean Sea of piracy; she had adopted and promoted Greek ideas of civilization; and she administered her empire with considerable skill, even if allowance is made for the inevitable graft. All of these accomplishments paved the way for the gospel to spread.

The picture in Palestine, however, was not so clear. A powerful Rome kept the lid on Jewish rebels who had strong religious and nationalistic feelings, while other Jews, Greek-thinking, tried to spread Greek culture. Palestine was a caldron. Hebrew was a language for scribes, who dominated interpretation of the law and Scripture. The people themselves spoke Aramaic and Greek, and many of them had to balance the scribes' interpretations against the struggle to survive. Judaism

The Roman road system was extensive. The ancient road shown opposite ran from Ephesus to the west into Syria and beyond to the east.

was a mosaic of differing views almost as complex as Christianity is today with its many denominations. Messiahs no longer were a phenomenon, and each one had his following. Differing groups promoted different political solutions to the land, ranging from passive acceptance of Rome to revolution. A Temple that may have been the largest religious complex in the world neared completion; but it had a high priesthood that was rejected by sizable numbers of Jews, such as the Essenes. Violence was common, generated by revolutionaries and by robber bands whose ranks were swelled by the massive unemployment that came about as Herod's building projects ended.

Amid the trauma of first-century Palestine, the people had a sense of expectancy that God was about to act. All of their ideas and programs for the Messiah's appearing were wrong—even the disciples could not or would not understand—yet throngs of people responded to Jesus' person and message, and, after his resurrection, they began to understand his messiahship.

Jesus lived and taught in a real land. That land—its cities, sites, and roads—is the subject of this book. Hopefully, it will help Christ's life to become more real and understandable.

All of the chapters, except those written by this editor, appeared earlier in *Biblical Illustrator*. I publically thank those authors who have allowed me to present their material in this new format. They are described briefly in the "Authors" section following the table of contents.

Photos are identified as to photographer and, if applicable, the museum location. Most photos are from the archives of *Biblical Illustrator*.

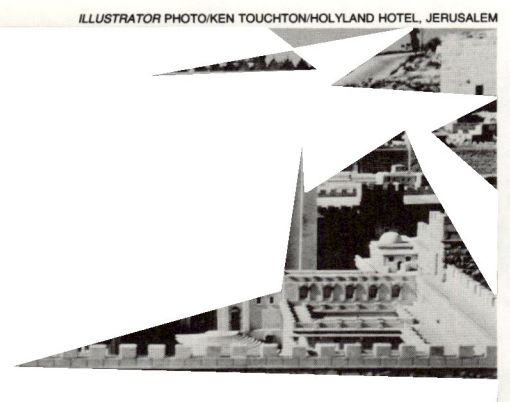

Scale model, located in Jerusalem, of Herod's Temple. It was among the most extensive of the ancient world.

The Scriptorium of Qumran, where the work of copying took place. Qumran was a monastery-type Essene community.

Special thanks go to Bill Latta, who designed the layout of this book. He was for several years the artist-designer of *Biblical Illustrator* and now supervises a section of artists of The Sunday School Board of the Southern Baptist Convention. He also did the isometric drawings of Herod's Temple and Qumran. We traveled together for weeks at a time to obtain most of the photos in this volume.

WILLIAM H. STEPHENS
Nashville, 1980

Modern Bethlehem in the hills of Judea south of Jerusalem. The Church of the Nativity is to the right.

Bethlehem

William H. Stephens

"But thou, Beth-lehem Eph-ra-tah, though thou be little among the thousands of Judah, yet out of thee shall come forth unto me that is to be ruler in Israel; whose goings forth have been from of old, from everlasting" (Mic. 5:2; see photos 1 and 2, p. 65; photo 7, p. 67).

From the time Micah spoke those words until now, only one person could conceivably be said to fulfill that prophecy: Jesus, the Son of Joseph and Mary. Not one person has been born in Bethlehem since Micah to challenge Jesus even for human, much less divine, leadership. It is for that incredible birth that Bethlehem is known today, and the reason that small city is the focus of pilgrimage for so many people.

The city was ancient when David was born there. He was the king the Jews in ancient times looked upon as an extraordinary leader who sought the will and way of God. Yet only a well points to David's origins in Bethlehem (though Ruth and Boaz stories cling to the traditional Shepherd's Field). Bethlehem is where Jesus was born, and for that she is remembered.

When we stand at a sacred site in the Holy Land, we cannot help but wonder, *Is this really the place?* Few sites are absolutely certain; but if the evidence eliminates reasonable doubt about a location, the visitor should enjoy the experience in confidence. The Church of the Nativity in Bethlehem is that sort of place; it is valid beyond reasonable doubt. An early church father named Justin referred about AD 100 to the cave where Jesus was born; another early Christian, Origen, referred to it about AD 248. Such early references indicate that Christians preserved the memory of the holy spot almost from the beginning of Christian history. The cave Justin and Origen referred to was desecrated by the Roman emperor Hadrian in AD 135 in an attempt to obliterate Christian worship. He erected a shrine there dedicated to Tammuz (Adonis), who was the lover of Aphrodite, the goddess of love. Al-

ILLUSTRATOR PHOTO/KEN TOUCHTON/VATICAN MUSEUM

Caesar Augustus, formerly called Octavian, was a masterful administrator.

CAPITOLINE MUSEUM, ROME

ILLUSTRATOR PHOTO/DAVID ROGERS

Top: Emperor Constantine built the first church structure over the nativity cave. *Bottom:* Present entrance to the cave.

most two centuries later, the converted Constantine won the empire and was proclaimed emperor. He declared Christianity to be the state religion and embarked on a program of commemorating the holy places in Palestine. He built the first commemorative church structure over the cave; his mother Helena dedicated it in AD 327. Excavations have uncovered some of Constantine's foundations and mosaics.

The Constantinian structure was destroyed in 529 by Samaritans during a revolt. Shortly afterward, about 531, Emperor Justinian built a larger structure. Though repaired and altered over the centuries, this building basically is the one that remains today.

Its survival is a bit of a miracle. Persians conquered Palestine early in the seventh century and systematically destroyed its church buildings. When they came to the Church of the Nativity, however, in 614, they saw the mosaics of the three Wise Men in Persian dress. So the building was allowed to stand because of a dress style.

The basilica has suffered various misfortunes over the centuries. Its marbles have been removed and it barely reflects its former glory. Evangelicals, however—who would prefer to see the cave in its original form—feel that the elaborate marble trappings and incense burners interfere with their worship at the site (see photo 3, p. 66).

Even so, to stand at the place where Jesus was born is a powerful experience. The Christian stands in awe as he stares at the fourteen-pointed silver star that claims to mark the very spot where Jesus was born (see photo 5 p. 68). The place of the manger is only a few feet away. It is covered with marble now, but the bare rock of the cave can be seen through a small opening.

The enormity of the act of God coming to man is sketched in bold strokes in that small chapel. There he lay, that tiny babe who was to change the world. To stand there in person in the very cave where that great event of incarnation—God coming to earth in the flesh—took place forces the heart to beat faster. The Christian's soul is flooded with a sense of victory and power, yet with humility and wonder. It is one of the great moments in a Holy Land pilgrimage.

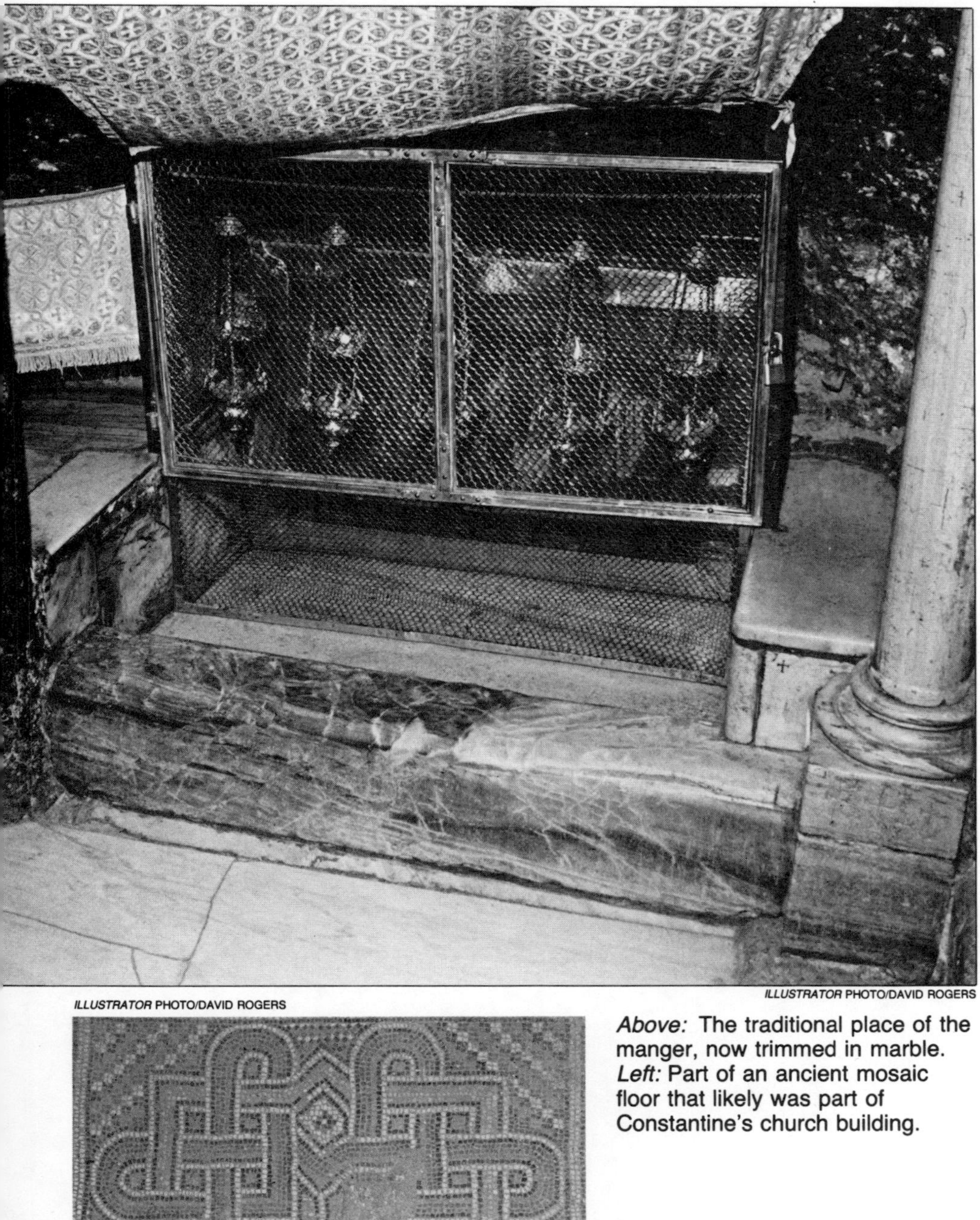

ILLUSTRATOR PHOTO/DAVID ROGERS

ILLUSTRATOR PHOTO/DAVID ROGERS

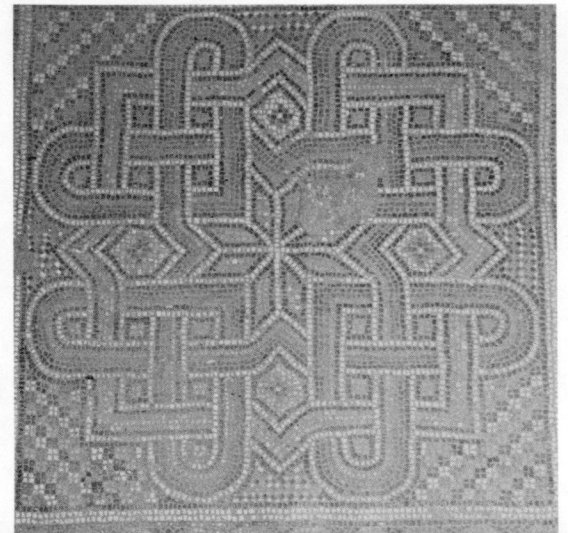

Above: The traditional place of the manger, now trimmed in marble. *Left:* Part of an ancient mosaic floor that likely was part of Constantine's church building.

ILLUSTRATOR PHOTO/DAVID ROGERS

The approach to the Church of the Nativity is rather dismal. You walk beside a long stone wall and through an ugly door that is so low you have to bend over to walk through it. That door, though, capsules the history of the basilica (see photo). Well above the opening is a long horizontal lintel. It marks the center massive doorway—there were three of them—built by Justinian. The large buttress that protrudes from the wall was built during the last century to support the weakening structure. Just above the current opening is an arch that marks a later doorway built by the Crusaders, who walled in the more massive opening. (The point at the top of the arch identifies it as built by the Crusaders.) Later, in order to keep people from riding their horses into the building, that doorway was crudely made smaller with the ugly unworked stones that form the current small opening.

The interior of the basilica is impressively ornate. The columns, made of red Bethlehem stone, may have been reused by Justinian from Constantine's earlier structure. Mosaics from the Crusader period have been preserved in the upper walls.

The cave (grotto) is reached by descending some steps to the right of the altar. The star and the manger are of most interest to Evangelicals, but the cave continues along the narrow passageway open to the "Room of St. Joseph," then to an altar and another side cave, the "Crypt of the Innocent Children." More authentic are the tombs connected to this part of the cave, those of Eusebius of Cremona, Paula, Eustochia, and Jerome. Jerome was the early church scholar who translated the Latin version of the Bible called the Vulgate (late fourth century AD). This translation became the official version of the Roman Catholic Church and is the translation on which the King James Version is primarily based. Jerome had his "office" in the Church of the Nativity.

The holiness of the nativity site attracted clerics over the centuries. Today Armenians, Greek Orthodox, and Roman Catholics share ownership—or watchcare—over the basilica and its complex of cloisters, monasteries, and basilicas. The famous bell tower is part of St.

ILLUSTRATOR PHOTO/KEN TOUCHTON

ILLUSTRATOR PHOTO/KEN TOUCHTON

Opposite: The tiny door to the Church of the Nativity was designed to keep horses out of the building. The arch above it was a Crusader doorway, while the large lintel, higher up, was built by Justinian. *Above, top:* The small door from inside the church.
Above: Entrance courtyard to the church.

Above, top: Traditional tomb of Rachel, near Bethlehem, cannot be authentic. *Above:* the fortress hill of the Herodium, six miles from Bethlehem.

Catherine's Church. During Christmas, which obviously is the season of greatest worship celebration in the Church of the Nativity, the three church groups commemorate the birth of Christ with elaborate processions and songs.

The traditional Shepherd's Field, so important in the Christmas story, is located less than a mile to the east of Bethlehem at *Deir er-Ra'ouat.* Excavations uncovered remains of a fifth-century church building, built over a cave. The site may or may not be the true one, since the area already was honored as the place where Jacob raised his flock and where Ruth and Boaz made their betrothal. Christians may have attached their own separate story to an already respected site. A modern shrine now commemorates the place. An alternate Shepherd's Field, *Siyar el-ghanam,* has no real claim to authenticity.

Bethlehem boasts other sites as well. The Herodium (see photo 2, p. 65), a palace fortress built by Herod the Great on top of the cone-shaped hill, is located beyond the Shepherd's Field. It can be seen from some distance away. Tekoa, Amos' home, is not far away. "Solomon's Pools" lie southeast; Pilate brewed considerable trouble for himself when he took money from the Temple treasury to build an aquaduct from these pools to Jerusalem. The very old monastery of Mar Saba clings to the desert cliffs of the Kidron Valley directly east of Bethlehem about halfway to the Dead Sea. Rachel's Tomb, which almost certainly is not authentic (she probably was buried at Ram north of Jerusalem; 1 Sam. 10:2), lies off the Jerusalem highway.

Appropriately, then, we begin our walk with Jesus at Bethlehem. From there, we should go to Egypt to recall the flight from Herod's wrath. Several sites on the way to and in Cairo, and up the Nile valley, claim to be spots where Joseph, Mary, and Jesus stayed, but they are only guesses. We will go next, then, to Nazareth, the hometown to which the holy family returned from Egypt.

ILLUSTRATOR PHOTO/DAVID ROGERS

ILLUSTRATOR PHOTO/KEN TOUCHTON

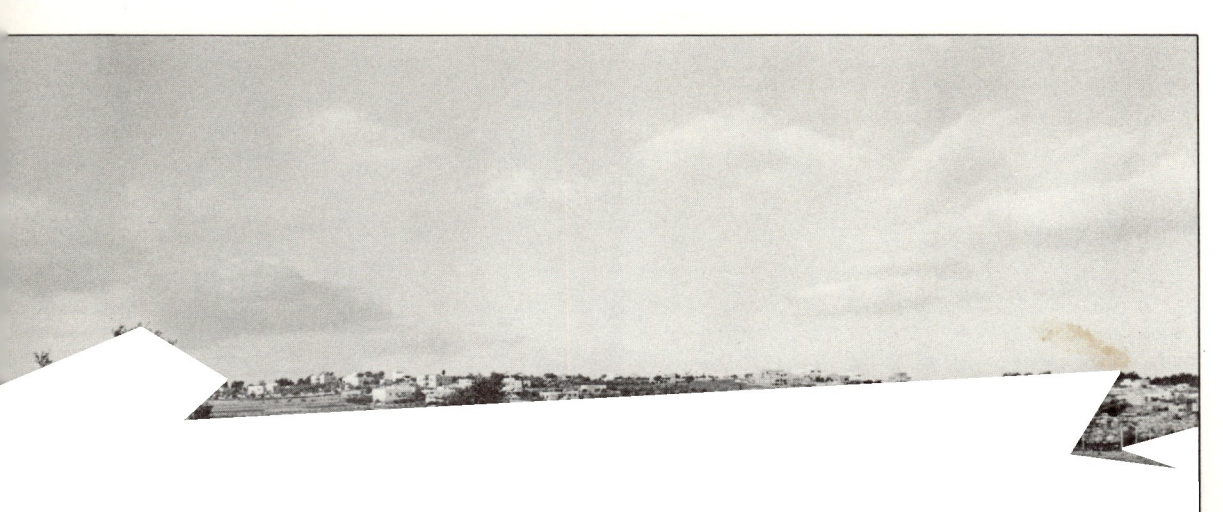

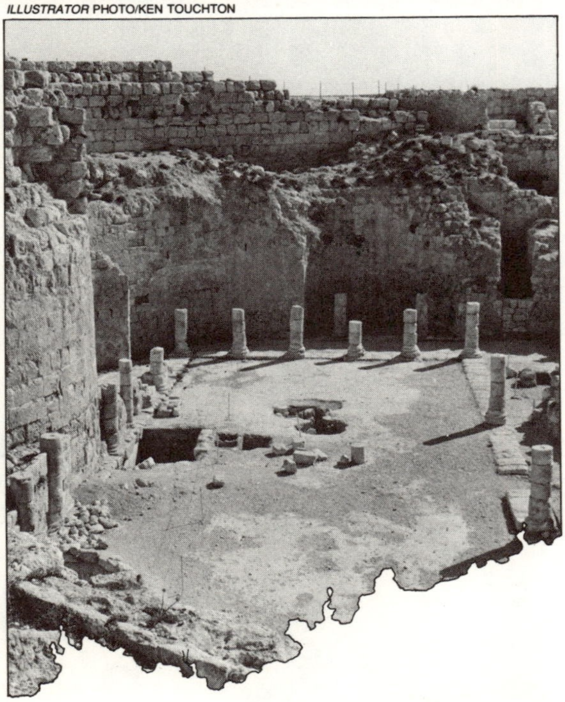

Above: One of the fields claimed to be the Shepherd's Field. *Left:* Interior ruins of Herod's Herodium.

Nazareth

Wayne Dehoney

The hill of Nazareth is on the southeast slope of the Carmel range, only twenty miles from caves where remains of prehistoric man have been found. The Nazareth hill also is honeycombed with ancient caves and tombs. However, limited excavations here indicated that human occupancy of Nazareth dates no earlier than 2000 BC. Most excavations have been of Roman Nazareth. That village of New Testament times was composed of small houses with flat roofs and caves cut out of the rock to provide storerooms (and often housing). The principal occupation apparently was agriculture.

A significant archeological discovery called the Nazareth Decree was found here. The inscription tablet was an "Ordinance of Caesar," declaring the violation or robbing of sealed graves to be a crime. This "tomb robbers' inscription" is sometimes suggested as one reason for the sealing of Christ's tomb and the stationing of Roman guards at the entrance. It was probably a general decree meant to control the notorious practice of grave-robbing.

Some scholars attribute the name *Nazareth* to the Hebrew root word for "watchtower." This interpretation is consistent with the evidence of a village of antiquity on the very crest of the hill, a watchtower overlooking a vast valley. From Jesus' time on, habitation had shifted downward on the slope of the hill.

The traditional Cave of the Annunciation, pointed out as the home of Mary and Joseph, where Gabriel's announcement took place.

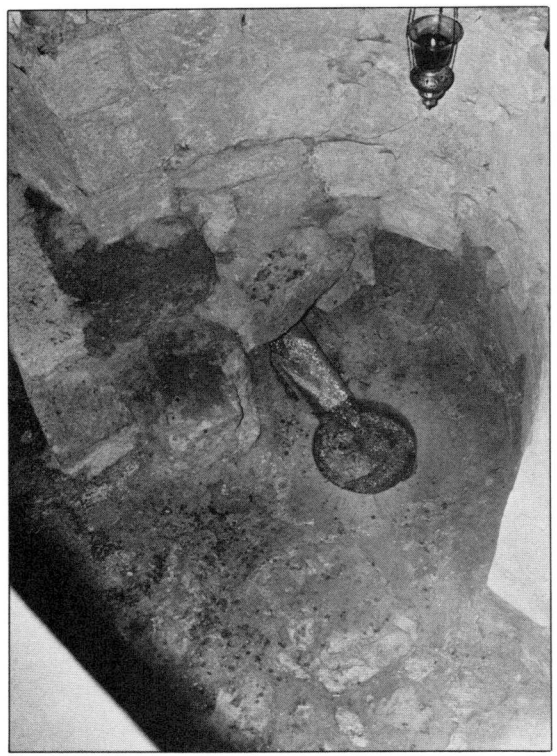

Two Mary's Wells are shown tourists. The one near the road is convenient, but this one, inside a church, is authentic.

The actual hill of Nazareth (altitude—1500 feet) rises five hundred feet above a broad valley that empties into the Plain of Esdraelon. This and the surrounding hills of Nazareth give us a key to the education of Jesus in history, in world outlook, and in natural beauty. From this high vantage point he could view a thirty-mile panorama unfolding in all directions, a veritable map of Old Testament history.

But Nazareth lay secluded in the hills six miles or more from the busy military and commercial routes that crisscrossed the sprawling village. Because of its "out-of-wayness," Nazareth was an insignificant village. No mention is made of it in the Old Testament, the Talmud, the Midrash, or in any writings by the Jewish historian Josephus. In fact, the earliest historical mention apart from the New Testament comes almost two hundred years after Christ. Speaking of Jesus, Philip said to Nathanael (John 1:45-46), "Can there any good thing come out of Nazareth?" This would not imply that a citizen of Nazareth was to be despised, but may have been merely the attitude of a polished city dweller toward the uncultivated rural people. To one who dwelt in Jerusalem, the center of Jewish religion and culture, a person from Galilee was from the boondocks. And someone from such an insignificant village as Nazareth would surely be a hayseed.

The history of Nazareth, even so, was bound up in the history of Galilee. The region was part of the Northern Kingdom of Israel that fell to Assyria in 722 BC. Much of the population, particularly the leaders and craftsmen, were deported out of the land. In turn, other conquered peoples were brought in to replace them. We have no idea of the resulting percentage of Gentile to Jew, but, at the least, the Jewish religion was infused with paganism (which, of course, was the cause of God's judgment in the first place).

The area that became Galilee was coveted by successive conquerors because it provided access to the Mediterranean Sea. Consequently, after Assyria fell, Babylon ruled the area, then Persia; then came Alexander the Great.

Alexander's cry of no more worlds to conquer

is well known; he died at the age of thirty-two after introducing immense change into the world. His top generals, though giving lip service to a unified empire, eventually divided it up among themselves. Some of them took the western regions. Ptolemy took Egypt, and Seleucus took Mesopotamia and Syria. The successors of the last two are referred to as Ptolemies and Seleucids.

Palestine was caught in a tug of war between the two dynasties. Generally speaking, the Ptolemies ruled for a long period after Alexander's death, then the Seleucids ruled for a long period, though the matter was not all that clearcut. Both dynasties, but especially the Selucids, put Palestine under pressure to take up Greek (Hellenistic) ways.

When the Maccabees led the Jews in revolt (see "Jerusalem," p. 95), beginning in 167 BC, they did not succeed in gaining the Galilee region. It was left to Aristobulus (104-103 BC) and Alexander Jannaeus (103-76 BC) to subdue the region after six hundred years of Gentile rule. Many Jews apparently lived in Galilee already, but Jannaeus forced many other inhabitants to convert to Judaism or be killed and, possibly, he resettled Jews from the south in Galilee.

Rome conquered Palestine in 63 BC; thus, Jewish independent rule lasted less than twenty years. Due to this history, the people of Galilee were much more influenced by Greek thought patterns than were the Jews of Judea. That is not to say that they were nonchalant in their faith. They had synagogues and rabbis, observed the laws, had messianic fervor, and their minority status for so long may have shaped in them a strong commitment to Judaism they would not otherwise have had. Even so, they lived more in the crosscurrents of history than did their average southern brother.

Sepphoris, however, was approximately four miles from Nazareth. It was an important city of Roman times, the provincial capital. Herod Antipas further beautified Sepphoris. Later he built Tiberias, but Sepphoris was his capital during most of Jesus' life.

The village of Nazareth in Jesus' day probably had a population of less than one thousand.

ILLUSTRATOR PHOTO/KEN TOUCHTON

An ancient, rebuilt synagogue claims to be the one in which Jesus worshiped. It is later, but captures an atmosphere.

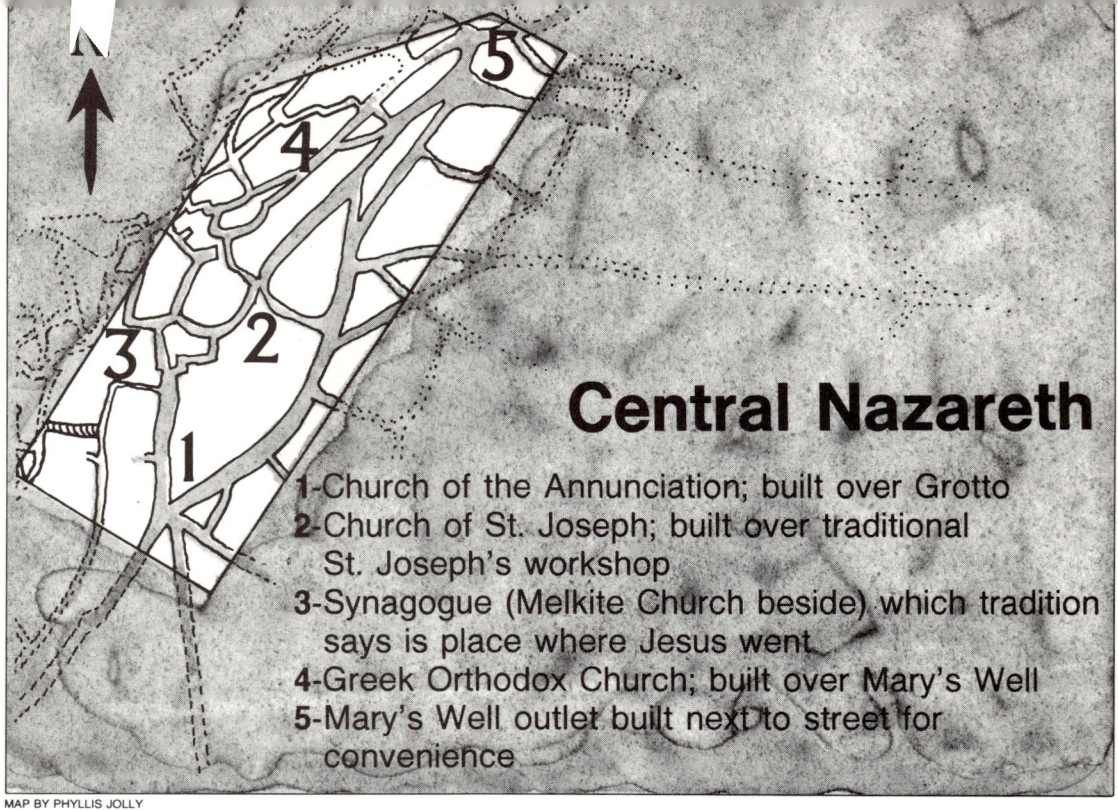

Central Nazareth

1 - Church of the Annunciation; built over Grotto
2 - Church of St. Joseph; built over traditional St. Joseph's workshop
3 - Synagogue (Melkite Church beside) which tradition says is place where Jesus went
4 - Greek Orthodox Church; built over Mary's Well
5 - Mary's Well outlet built next to street for convenience

MAP BY PHYLLIS JOLLY

Today its population exceeds thirty thousand with a large population of Arab Greek Orthodox Christians. The city is less than 20 percent Moslem. It is a city of stone houses, markets, shops, cactus hedges, and a variety of trees: fig, olive, orange, pomegrante, and cypress. Israelis have settled an adjoining area they call New Nazareth.

The only authentic site that dates back to the time of Jesus is Mary's Well, over which the Greek Orthodox Church of St. Gabriel is constructed. In this beautiful church building, the spring (which is Nazareth's only natural source of water) gushes forth and flows some distance to an outside fountain, which is often pointed out to tourists as Mary's Well since it is handy to the tour bus route. It is a beautiful sight to see a Palestinian woman lift a jar of water to her head and walk away from the well under the heavy load in a swinging pace of ease and grace, reenacting today the scenes in which Mary must have participated many times.

No solid archeological evidence authenticates other sites, but they do objectify the traditions of the Nazareth story. The Roman Catholic Church of the Annunciation is built over a traditional cave of the annunciation regarded as the home of Mary and Joseph. The present building, constructed on earlier Byzantine and Crusader foundations, is the largest Christian church edifice in the Middle East. It was completed in 1969.

At another site, the Church of St. Joseph (built in 1914) claims to be constructed over Joseph's carpenter shop. The caves, cisterns, silos, and

Above: Traditional, but too far away, Hill of the Precipice. *Above, right:* modern Nazareth.

winepresses uncovered on this site do give a graphic impression of conditions of Jesus' day. Nazareth was a forested area which provided an abundance of raw materials for the carpenter. Finished products found a ready market in the nearby capital of Sepphoris. Even to this day there is a similar family relationship where the sons of olive wood workers learn the trade from their fathers. It is interesting that Jesus, the boy who worked with the wood in the carpenter shop with Joseph, would someday be crucified on a tree.

A Melchite Church in the market area is next to the site that claims to be the ancient synagogue where Jesus went to school and where he preached. Jesus studied the Scriptures in the synagogue, apparently with a photographic memory and brilliant mind that enabled him, at twelve years of age, to confound the Temple scholars in Jerusalem at the Passover season. A visit to this church is a fascinating experience because of the adjacent market. Automobiles are not allowed in the narrow lanes which are filled with heavily laden donkeys and pressing people and sidewalk shops of merchandise and food.

On the outskirts of Nazareth to the south is a precipice, the traditional site where the people of Nazareth threatened to cast Christ down headlong. A Marionite Christian Church nearby memorializes this event.

When the Roman general Titus ravaged Jerusalem and dispersed the Jews in AD 70, many found refuge in Galilee. A priestly family named Pisces settled in Nazareth and the city became a secondary center of Jewish influence for the next three centuries. It seems that only Jews were permitted to live in Nazareth during this time. Not until after AD 324, when Emperor Constantine built the first Church of the Annunciation, did Nazareth become a significant Christian center.

Thus this insignificant, inconsequential agricultural village, hidden in the hills apart from the mainstream of humanity and completely overlooked in ancient history, finds its sole claim to fame and continuing historical significance as the boyhood home of Jesus, often called the "Nazarene."

Sepphoris: Capital of Galilee

Dan G. Kent

Sepphoris, located near Jesus' home of Nazareth, was the capital of Galilee during most of Jesus' earthly life. The city enjoyed a relatively high altitude. It became one of the largest and most strongly fortified cities in Galilee. Because it was perched on top of a mountain, the Hebrews called it *Sepphoris,* which means "birds." Even at that early time, it was the administrative capital of Galilee. Though never mentioned in the Bible, Jesus must have walked its streets many times.

The city dates to the second century BC. It was mentioned for the first time during the period between the Testaments, at the beginning of the reign of Alexander Jannaeus, one of the Hasmonaean kings. (The Hasmoneans, also called Maccabees, led the Jewish revolt against the Greeks and ruled Judea until the Roman conquest.) Even in its beginning Sepphoris was important and was part of a violent, stormy pattern. It was first mentioned because it was attacked by Ptolemy Latyrus. The year was 103 BC.

Sepphoris has only been peripherally excavated. These circular stones may be remains of a church building.

Pompey was the general who conquered Palestine for the Roman Empire. Gabinius was the Roman proconsul of Syria in 57-55 BC who carried out Pompey's administrative arrangements for the conquered areas. Gabinius was harsh on the Jewish people. He allowed the Samaritans to become independent; he separated Galilee from Judea; he split the Jewish state into five districts called *synedria*. He designated Sepphoris the capital of the shrunken district of Galilee. These synedria were dissolved after a short time, but Sepphoris continued to have a prominent place.

By the time of Julius Caesar, an Idumean (see "Jerusalem," p. 95) named Antipater actually

ILLUSTRATOR PHOTO/KEN TOUCHTON

was ruling the land for Rome. He appointed his younger son, Herod, to be governor of Galilee, even though this one who came to be known as Herod the Great was still only a boy. Later, when Antipater was murdered by one of his opponents in 43 BC, Herod and his brothers were appointed rulers over all of Judea. An invasion by Parthians, an empire from the east, forced Herod to leave Palestine and flee to Rome. While there he won appointment as king of the Jews.

But Herod had to fight for every inch of the land the Roman senate had awarded him. He retook Sepphoris during a snowstorm in the winter of 39-38 BC. It continued as the capital of Galilee.

Herod the Great died in 4 BC. Emperor Augustus eventually divided the kingdom among Herod's three surviving sons. The son named Herod Antipas was given Galilee. This is the Herod of most New Testament references.

Augustus had foreseen the unrest that would come with the elder Herod's death, and come it did. Herod the Great had been able to suppress the Jewish nationalists (later called Zealots) for a time, but now they revolted in a violent and bitter, but futile, effort to be free of outside control. Guerrilla-like bands of these patriot extremists appeared throughout the countryside. Josephus called them robbers, but to the Jewish people they were heroes. One such band, led by Judas of Galilee, captured Sepphoris. He pillaged the royal palace and armed his followers from the royal arsenal.

Augustus ordered Varus, the governor of Syria, into Palestine. With an army of twenty thousand men, Varus destroyed hundreds of towns, crucified two thousand rebels, and sold thirty thousand Jews into slavery. Sepphoris was one of the towns that was conquered and destroyed. Its people were enslaved. We don't know what Judas's fate was, but Acts 5:37 indicates that he perished.

All of this occurred when Jesus was a boy in Nazareth, four miles to the south of Sepphoris. He knew well the entire tragic story. Perhaps he even saw the rows of crosses that lined the highway and on which hung the crucified bodies. If so, his willingness to go to the cross is even more incredible.

Herod Antipas rebuilt Sepphoris into a magnificent city. Jesus' family may well have taken part in the reconstruction. Carpenters and masons from nearby Nazareth helped rebuild the homes, markets, and food shops, and they worked on the hillside theater and the aqueduct. Archeologists have uncovered these and other ruins. The elaborate aqueduct system, tunnel, and reservoirs supplied the city with water from a spring a mile away.

Herod Antipas later built Tiberias on the shore of the lake of Galilee to be his new capi-

A castle with walls 12 feet thick dominates the site where the Crusaders camped prior to their disastrous defeat in 1187 at Hattin.

ILLUSTRATOR PHOTO/KEN TOUCHTON

ILLUSTRATOR PHOTO/KEN TOUCHTON
An almost-covered arch on the periphery of the tell. Ruins date from Hellenistic to Arab periods.

tal, but Sepphoris remained, along with Tiberias, one of the two chief centers of Gentile influence in lower Galilee.

A well-traveled road followed the Turan Valley from the Mediterranean coast past Sepphoris to Tiberias. Grain was transported over this road from east of the lake to the seaports. Farmers led their donkeys, loaded down with grapes or vegetables, to the markets of this commercial and agricultural center. No doubt, Jesus walked that same way himself during his journeys about Galilee.

Sepphoris was a part of the kingdom of Agrippa I, grandson of Herod the Great, who reigned from AD 37-44. After his death, Emperor Claudius returned it to the rule of the Roman procurators. One of these procurators, Felix (AD 52-60), reaffirmed Sepphoris as the capital of Galilee and granted it autonomy. Many prominent priestly families lived there in the latter part of the first century. Sepphoris even became a center of Jewish learning. The Sanhedrin was located there at one time.

When the general Jewish revolt against Rome broke out in AD 66, the rebels set up a formal government in Jerusalem. They divided the country into seven military districts, each with its own commander. The most exposed of these posts, the command of Galilee, was given to a young priest with no previous military experience named Joseph. He later came to be known as Flavius Josephus.

Josephus fortified the city against the coming Roman attack, but the people of Sepphoris were loyal to the Romans. They surrendered without resistance and cooperated with the Romans in subjugating the rest of Galilee.

To quell the uprising Nero sent Vespasian, his best general, into Palestine. He easily conquered Galilee and sent his son Titus to complete the capture of Judea and Jerusalem. Sepphoris became the home for refugees from the southern areas.

With Jerusalem being destroyed by Titus in AD 70 and the widespread Jewish revolt brought to an end, Sepphoris was given to Agrippa II. It eventually became a Christian community.

The site of Sepphoris was excavated peripherally in 1931 by L. Waterman and S. Yeivin in an expedition sponsored by the University of Michigan. Some archeological work also was done there by E. L. Sukenik. The site is called Zippori today, while the nearby village is called a similar name. In 1970 the village had 265 inhabitants.

Sepphoris is a place little known now, even among those of us who count Palestine as a holy land. Yet it was an integral part of the background and daily life of Jesus. A study of Sepphoris gives us a sampling of the swirling, complicated currents that made up the religious, economic, political, and social life of the real people of New Testament times.

ILLUSTRATOR PHOTO/KEN TOUCHTON

ILLUSTRATOR PHOTO/KEN TOUCHTON

Top: Scattered blocks, columns, and rubble dot the site. *Bottom:* A stairway, over which blocks were later laid.

The Road from Nazareth to Jerusalem

Wayne Dehoney

It is eighty miles south from Nazareth to Jerusalem.

From the very beginning, our journey was an exciting mixture of the ancient and modern. Crowds of pressing, hurrying people filled the street, impatient truckers grated their horns, camel bells tinkled, and Arab boys urgently cried, "Eee, Eee," as they prodded the burdened donkeys through the crowd.

Coming out of Nazareth, the road breaks downhill into a valley that opens into the vast Plain of Esdraelon (Jezreel, Megiddo; see photos 8 and 10, pp. 70-71). This is the rich, flat granary and breadbasket of Galilee that stretches for more than twenty miles in all directions. We are driving the route Jesus walked on his boyhood journey to Jerusalem so we can recall the places where great events occurred, places Jesus himself passed on his journey.

On the left looms the most conspicuous mountain in Galilee, Mount Tabor with its dome-shaped summit, the traditional site of the tranfiguration. Just beyond is Endor, where the ghost of Samuel surprised the witch and appeared so he could answer Saul on the eve of battle (1 Sam. 28:7-14). A bit further to the south and on the left is Nain, where Christ raised the widow's son from the dead.

Speeding along the blacktop road we quickly pass through the crossroads Arab village of Afula in the heart of the valley. Two miles further we pass on the left a small hill called "Little Mt. Hermon." On its slopes is Shunem, where lived a "great woman" and her husband who kept a guest room for the tired Elisha. Here the prophet restored to life her son who had died of heat prostration. Three miles further on the right is the little Arab village of Yizreel, site of ancient Jezreel (See photo 10, p. 71). Here Ahab built a palace; here his pagan wife Jezebel

ILLUSTRATOR PHOTO/KEN TOUCHTON

Modern Nablus, nestled by Mts. Ebal and Gerizim and near ancient Shechem.

had Naboth stoned because he refused to sell his vineyard to Ahab; here Jehu had Jezebel thrown from the palace window to her death; and here the heads of Ahab's seventy sons were displayed at the gate of the city after their execution.

Elsewhere we see the lushness of this productive green valley. The rainfall and climate produce two crops a year of wheat, barley, tomatoes, peppers, and cabbage. Far to the east is Mount Gilboa, scene of Saul's last battle with the Philistines in which he and Jonathan were killed and after which David became king.

Our first stop is at Jenin, a modern Arab town that sits squarely on the eastern edge of the great Esdraelon plains. A tradition claims that here Jesus cured the ten lepers—and only one returned to thank him (Luke 17:11-18). Here we buy luscious oranges (not grown in Jesus' day) and a delicious mutton shish kebab from a sidewalk vendor who is cooking on a charcoal brazier fashioned from half of a five-gallon tin gasoline can.

We leave Jenin to enter the quiet, brown hills of Samaria that lie as a buffer between Galilee and Judea. A low-lying tell to the west, five miles out, is ancient Dothan. (A tell is a mound-shaped hill built up as a succeeding series of towns are destroyed.) Here Elisha saw the hills filled with chariots of fire during the Syrian siege. God delivered the city (2 Kings 6:13-24). The valley that stretches to the right is a main caravan route from Damascus to Egypt. Here Joseph was seized by his jealous brothers, thrown into a well, and later sold into slavery to the Midianites (Gen. 37:14-17). Today it is not unusual to see a string of camels laden with merchandise pass along this same caravan route.

Thirteen miles further along to the east is the hill of Samaria, where the ancient capital of the Northern Kingdom was located. This great natural fortress rises 350 feet above the plain. Walking amid these ruins that span the centuries we pick up a chip of mosaic and touch a world that is thousands of years old, one that spans the Hebrew, Greek, and Roman eras. What bloodstained chapters of history were written on

ILLUSTRATOR PHOTO/KEN TOUCHTON

ILLUSTRATOR PHOTO/KEN TOUCHTON

ILUSTRATOR PHOTO/DAVID ROGERS

Top: Mt. Tabor, important in Israel's history, the traditional but inaccurate Mount of Transfiguration. *Middle:* Dothan, near where Joseph was sold into slavery. *Bottom:* An eroded hill in Samaria.

this hill! Here soldiers washed the blood of Ahab from his chariot; here Jezebel slew the prophets of Jehovah; and here several years later Jehu slaughtered the prophets of Baal. Here Mariamne, the murdered wife of Herod, haunted the king, and here in his golden palace Herod strangled his two sons.

Isaiah called the land of Samaria the "pride of Ephraim." Looking from this hill at the cornfields and the secluded vales and the winding streams that flash in the sun and the groves of olive trees and terraced fields that stretch in all directions, we find justification for Isaiah's pride!

ILLUSTRATOR PHOTO/DAVID ROGERS

Monumental steps once led to the Temple of Augustus, part of Herod's great building campaign in ancient Samaria to honor the emperor who gave him the city. The temple is the highest point.

Continuing on toward Jerusalem, we come to Nablus, today a village of fanatical Moslems. In this narrow pass between the mountains are two natural amphitheaters facing each other. It was here that the dramatic reciting of the blessings and the curses of the law took place (Josh. 24). Here Joshua recited all the things that God had done for the children of Israel and then said, "As for me and my house, we will serve the Lord" (v. 15).

Up on the slopes of Mount Gerizim on the right, amid the narrow twisting streets and crowded houses of Nablus, is a Samaritan synagogue and colony. The high priest claims to be a direct descendant of Aaron. The priest shows us the great treasure of this last remnant of these ancient biblical people, a Samaritan Codex of the Pentateuch. This precious scroll is kept in a silver case wrapped in faded green fabric and is proudly displayed as "written by the very hand of Aaron himself."

This land is full of the memories of Abraham, Isaac, and Jacob. Just beyond Nablus on the left is Jacob's Well, an authentic site. The debris of the centuries has filled in above the well. Descending a flight of steps, we come to the very curbstones where Jesus sat and talked with the Samaritan woman (John 4). The shaft still is deep and a priest draws the rope to bring water up sixty feet in a small bucket. We drink it with a beautiful memory of Christ talking to the woman at this very site about the "living water."

As we continue south through the hills of Samaria, we pass through tortuous, twisting valleys where every hill is marked with ghosts of ancient terraces. In the time of Christ these hills were covered with figs, olives, and vines. The blacktop road now is up, then down, rising and falling in a series of double hairpin curves, twisting through the rocky hills.

Unconsciously, the people illustrate the Bible on every hand. One man guides a primitive plow drawn by an ox and a camel through a rocky field. The wooden yoke drops from the high camel to the low ox so that the ox seems to bear more than his share of the weight. Perhaps this is what Paul meant when he said, "Be ye

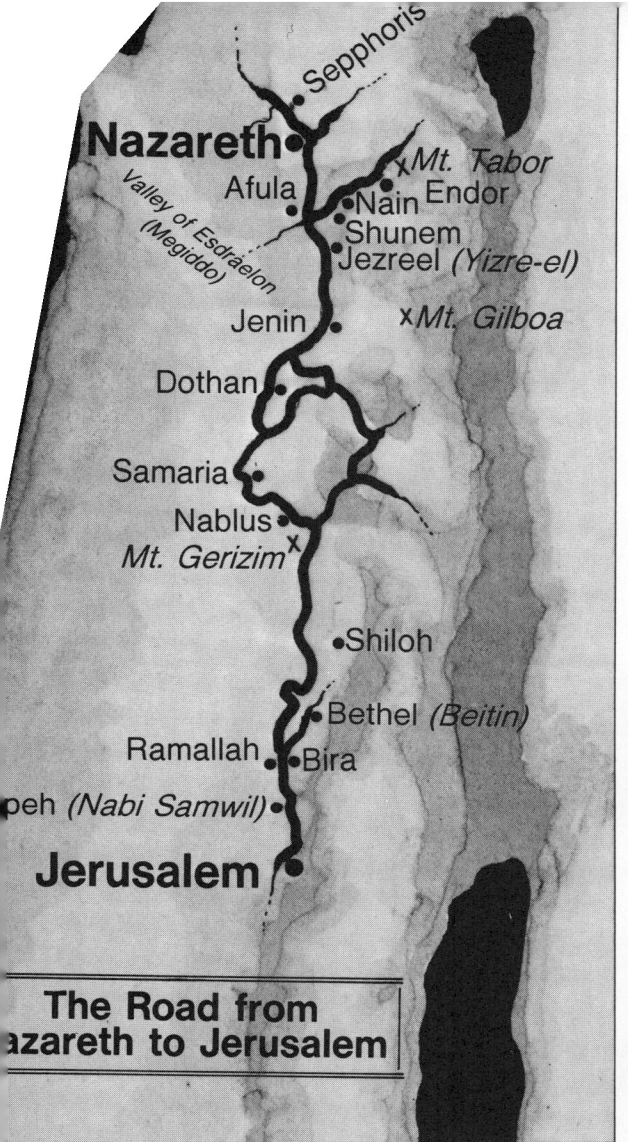

The Road from Nazareth to Jerusalem

MAP BY PHYLLIS JOLLY

Jacob spent his first night with a stone for a pillow and dreamed of a golden angel's stairway to heaven.

Nine miles out of Jerusalem, we pass between the twin cities of Ramallah and Bira. The country to the right is Gibeon, rich in Old Testament history and the site of the Gibeonites' deceit of Joshua (Josh. 9).

ILLUSTRATOR PHOTO/DAVID ROGERS

ILLUSTRATOR PHOTO/DAVID ROGERS

Top: Remains of a Crusader fortress and scattered ruins at Bethel. *Bottom:* Small mosque built from reused Hellenistic stones.

not unequally yoked together with unbelievers" (2 Cor. 6:14). Girls with five-gallon gasoline cans of water on their heads (instead of the jars of yesterday) walk through the fields of growing barley, while little boys drive herds of goat and sheep across the rocky fields.

There are holy memories all along the way. Shiloh lies in a valley on the left, ancient Israel's sanctuary. Further along and back in the rocky hills is Bethel, where the lonely, runaway lad

Arab structures among the excavations that uncovered ruins and artifacts dating back to 3000 BC. At Gibeon, Solomon prayed for wisdom.

Excavations have revealed an ancient camping spot at Ramallah with abundant springs, allowing the possibility of a tradition being true that the family of Jesus stopped here on their return from the Temple only to discover that the boy was not with them (Luke 2:41-50).

Beyond and to the right we pass a large tell where extensive excavations have uncovered what may be ancient Mizpeh, where Samuel erected a stone and "called the name of it Eben-ezer, saying, Hitherto hath the Lord helped us" (1 Sam. 7:12). The phrase of the song "Here I raise mine Ebenezer," is a reference to that event.

Then the sight of the Jerusalem airport brings us back to the reality of the twentieth century. Breaking over the high hill five miles northwest of Jerusalem, we see the domes and towers of Jerusalem the Golden. As the scene bursts on us, we stand in silence and gaze on the magnificence of the Holy City spread out before us. It is an awesome mixture of the sacred and secular, the ancient and modern, of a past filled with glory and revelation, with a present torn by dynamic conflict and tension. Moreover, it is the symbol of a future promise of a "new Jerusalem coming down out of heaven," fashioned by the hand of God himself! Jesus' first glimpse of the city surely was as impressive. And all along the way from Nazareth to Jerusalem he saw the hills and valleys and towns where wars were fought and prophets walked and God spoke. He was the divine Son of God, and he grew up surrounded by the history of God.

Ramallah (left) and Bira (above), twin cities where Jesus' family may have stopped when they discovered he was not with them.

John the Baptist

William H. Stephens

Above: Ain Karim, the traditional birthplace of John, dominated by the Church of St. John. Other churches commemorate John and his parents. *Opposite, top:* Traditional cave (note rock ceiling) where John was born. *Opposite, bottom:* Wilderness of Judea.

By the time Jesus began his ministry, Joseph was dead. No one knows how long Jesus, as the eldest son, served as head of the family before his baptism. However, probably at age thirty Jesus began his ministry by being baptized by John.

John the Baptist was six months older than his cousin Jesus. Because of this age difference and the importance of age thirty during that period of history, along with comparing evidence from the Bible and from secular sources, we may reasonably assume that John began his ministry six months before he baptized Jesus, probably in AD 28-29. Some scholars believe John was orphaned early and was raised by the Qumran community, the Essene sect that produced the Dead Sea Scrolls. Qumran was a monastic community near the Dead Sea; the Essenes were a strict sect who were preparing for the coming of the Messiah.

He may have been raised by them. But, if so, he went his own way, for his preaching reflects important differences from the teachings of Essenes. The Essenes looked for a messiah called the "Teacher of Righteousness"; John also looked for a messiah. The belief that the messiah's coming was very close permeated the minds of the Jews of the first century; many ideas existed as to who that messiah might be. Some thought he would be a human deliverer like David; others thought he would be divine; still others thought he would be human but endued with God's power in a miraculous way. So far as we know, all of those who believed in the coming messiah thought he would be a military conqueror. Even John thought so.

John's preaching, then, fell on ready ears. His preaching made sense. Repentance surely had to precede the arrival of the chosen one. John's powerful preaching drew large followings and his reputation increased. A band of disciples

ILLUSTRATOR PHOTO/KEN TOUCHTON

grew around him, yet John never allowed them to think he was the messiah to come. Thus, when John baptized Jesus and announced to his disciples that they should follow him, most of them accepted his word.

John preached and baptized in many places, including Samaria and Transjordan (the region east of the Jordan River). Jesus went to John, though, when John was baptizing in the Jordan River and "preaching in the wilderness of Judea," (Matt. 3:1). The region of that name lies between Jerusalem and the Jordan and extends south through the region west of the Dead Sea, an area that includes Qumran (see photo 9, p. 70). This description would give some support to the fact that John at least felt some kinship with Qumran.

The wilderness of Judea was symbolic of religious purity—both as a separation from the sins of the society and as an image of the wilderness wanderings after the Exodus from Egypt. John's preaching there was a logical matter; even so, his way of life and prophetic speaking must have been quite impressive for people to make the long, tiring journey to hear him. Such a response by large numbers of people also reveals how powerful was the conviction that the messiah was about to appear. Even tax collectors(!) came to hear him. But so did soldiers—and these may have been Jewish revolutionaries rather than Romans, whose practices sometimes were lawless even toward their own countrymen.

These teachings of John were more revolutionary than they first appeared to be. John called people back to the terms of the covenant made at Sinai and in the wilderness. Luke 3:10-14 reveals something of the ethical demands, the caring of persons for one another, that the Sinai covenant called for. His statements recorded by Matthew 3:7-10 called for true repentance and right living; he sounded

ILLUSTRATOR PHOTO/KEN TOUCHTON

37

very much like an Amos. The kind of changes John called for were radical, indeed. And, his perception of who were true Israelites is a forecast of the inclusion of Gentiles into the chosen people of God.

Jesus' ministry began in the shadow of John's. At first, Jesus' ministry paralleled John's. Like John, Jesus preached repentance and the arrival of the kingdom of God. Soon, however, Jesus' ministry took its own direction.

Probably during the second year of Jesus ministry, John was imprisoned because he made embarrassing public pronouncements against Herod Antipas' act of marrying his sister-in-law Herodias. Herod had John imprisoned at Machaerus, east of the upper end of the Dead Sea, and finally beheaded him during a moment of lecherous drunkenness at the request of Salome. So ended the earthly life of this prophet whom Jesus designated as the one who was to prepare the way for the Messiah; John was the

Machaerus, where John was beheaded.

fulfillment of Micah's prophecy (3:1; 4:5).

Jesus' act of submitting to John's baptism had several facets: He endorsed John's teaching and work; he identified himself with the kingdom John announced; he identified himself with sinful humanity; he set an example for all believers to follow; and the occasion marked a public announcement of the beginning of his ministry. That great event likely took place somewhere along the southern part of the Jordan River.

DRAWING OF QUMRAN'S ESSENE COMPLEX BY BILL LATTA

Drawing of Qumran, by Bill Latta, shows something of the life of the community. Was John raised here as some scholars contend?

The Wilderness of John's Baptizing

A. Stuart Arnold

How can the word *wilderness* be applied to a river valley where the water flows year-round? Strangely enough, that is an accurate description of the valley of the river Jordan, whose banks were the scene of John the Baptist's ministry.

To the north, from its origins at Banias down to the Sea of Galilee and further south to Beth-shean, the Jordan valley is fertile and of great beauty. But further south, the Jordan flows through forbidding and barren country. But it was not always so. Biblical scholars of the last century—including even the great George Adam Smith—remarked on the absence of any significant towns and cities in the valley. More recently, Nelson Glueck and the staffs of the Smithsonian Institution and of the American Schools of Oriental Research have shown that this valley once had a thriving population. Glueck examined seventy sites where towns used to stand, many of them as long ago as six thousand years. Their number declined in the years following the conquest of the land by the Israelites, fewer than half of the towns still were in existence. During the New Testament period the two cities of any size were Jericho to the south and Scythopolis (ancient Beth-shean) where the Plain of Jezreel spills down into the valley (see photo 25, p. 108).

The distance from the Sea of Galilee to the Dead Sea is only sixty-five miles, but the length of the river's course between the points is two hundred miles. The Jordan winds backward and forward in its course, unusual for a river that flows between mountain ranges and falls rather quickly.

The river that John saw was about ninety feet wide and had a depth of from three to ten feet. It was difficult to cross in places where the current was treacherous and fast, but a number of fords provided safe crossings for travelers. John likely baptized at these fords. Along each bank of the river the water produced a wealth of thick vegetation. The fertile band was not very wide, but it

ILLUSTRATOR PHOTO/KEN TOUCHTON

The wilderness was symbolic to Israel because of the forty years of wandering. The photo is area southeast of Jerusalem, west of Dead Sea.

was a jungle of tamarisk, willow, and broom trees with clumps of bamboo, acacia, and thorn growing in the exceedingly hot climate. In former times these thickets sheltered many animals, including lions, where jackals and hyenas hunt today.

As John looked up from the waters he would have seen the hills of Galilee to the west and the mountains of Gilead to the east. The hills of both ranges rose from 200 to 1500 feet above the valley floor. Sometimes the hills are only 2 miles apart with the Jordan flowing in between (as at a point ten miles south of Beth-shean); at other times they open to a plain 12 or 14 miles wide (as at Jericho). The river snakes its way across the sandy floor between the white marl hills, sometimes reaching the lower slopes to the west and then flowing back to the foot of the Gileads in the east.

Where, along this terrain that twists for two hundred miles, is the spot where Jesus was baptized? We have no precise answer to that question. Biblical evidence is slight and traditions are contradictory.

John 3:23 mentions Aenon near Salim as one place where John baptized. *Aenon* means "full of springs," chosen by John for baptizing by immersion because there was an adequate supply of water there. The traditional location since at least the time of Eusebius (a fourth century Christian scholar) is at Salim, a few miles south of Beth-shean on the west side of the river. The Madeba map, a mosaic on the floor of a seventh-century church in Jordan, conflicts with this view. It shows Aenon on the east bank of the river.

The Wilderness of John's Baptizing

MAP BY PHYLLIS JOLLY

ILLUSTRATOR PHOTO/DAVID ROGERS

Tell Beth-shean, ancient city that controlled an east-west route from the Megiddo Valley to a Jordan crossing, a possible site of John's baptizing.

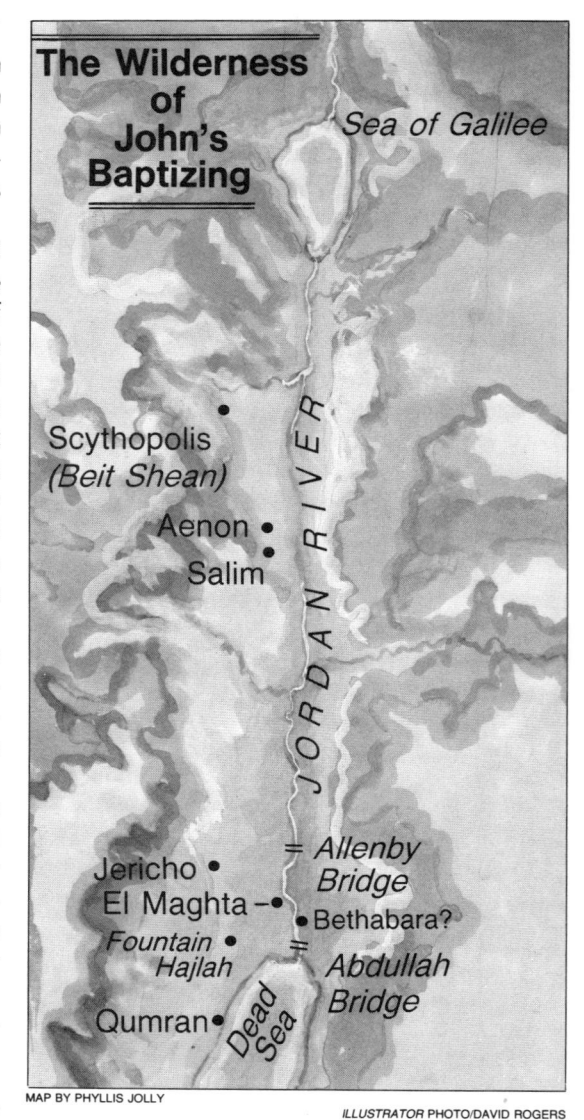

The conflict need not occupy us too much because Jesus likely was baptized at another place of John's labor. While the King James Version records that Jesus was baptized by John at Bethabara (John 1:28), early manuscripts of this reference have "Bethany beyond Jordan." This Bethany is a different town than the Bethany where Mary, Martha, and Lazarus lived. "Beyond Jordan" refers to the east side of Jordan. Did another Bethany exist in New Testament times, across the river on its eastern side? Origen (a Christian theologian of the late second and early third centuries who lived at Caesarea), tried to answer that question. Evidently, he never made the journey to the possible area, but he made diligent inquiries and was unable to find any location bearing that name. (Succeeding generations of scholars have been no more successful.) The tradition Origen picked up appears to have been well-established already, that Jesus was baptized at Bethabara, a village on the eastern bank of the river. This place-name crept into some versions of John's Gospel, and the King James Version, which did not have the benefit of many manuscripts found since, says that Jesus was baptized at Bethabara. Since "Bethabara" is found in some old Syriac and Sahidic (a dialect from the Memphis area of Egypt) versions, this tradition must have been widespread even in the earliest days. Without question, though, the best and oldest manuscripts read "Bethany beyond Jordan."

We really are no better off if we accept Origen's suggestion, for no one knows where Bethabara is. That location is just as uncertain as Bethany beyond Jordan! Bethabara means simply "the place of crossing." In the eighth century Arculf described a cross that stood in the river at the supposed place of the baptism. A rope reached from it to the bank so that pilgrims could bathe in the center of the stream. On the shore, at the place where tradition said Jesus laid his clothes, stood a church and the Monastery of St. John. In the nineteenth century Roman Catholics identified the ford near the ruins of the monastery as the place of baptism. Greek Christians hallowed a place some two or three miles downstream. Others have tried to

The traditional and celebrated site of John's baptizing, not far north of the Dead Sea. A major road crossed near here from Jerusalem to Amman.

Above: Jordan Valley, looking northwest from Jericho. John likely preached at points all along the valley. *Opposite:* A portion of the Madeba mosaic map of the sixth century that shows the traditional sites for John's ministry; the writing is Greek.

link the place of Jesus' baptism with the place where Joshua's armies crossed the river dry-footedly on their entry into the Promised Land (Josh. 3:1-17). These places are a few miles north of the Dead Sea and east of the river.

Another view of the location of Bethabara is suggested by *The Westminster Bible Dictionary*. If the reading of Bethabara is accepted, it is suggested that the location of a ford at 'Abarah, twelve miles south of the lake of Galilee, would fit the story better than the more southerly location. The events that followed the baptism, according to John's Gospel, took place in Galilee. John, however, does not include the story of the temptation of Jesus. The first three Gospels all place this event immediately after the baptism. Tradition holds that the wilderness of Jesus' temptation was above Jericho, which supports the southerly theory.

Since neither the site of Bethany beyond Jordan nor the one of Bethabara are known, we have only tradition to give clues to the right location. Tradition holds that the point on the river known as *el Hajlah,* midway between the Abdullah Bridge and the Allenby Bridge, is the most likely place. In earlier days hundreds of pilgrims sought to visit the traditional site and to enter the waters in an attempt to express their devotion to the Lord. Today it is quite common for Baptist groups touring the Holy Land to hold baptismal services in the Jordan (usually at a convenient place where the river leaves the lake of Galilee). Though it is good for us to try to use every means to get nearer to our Lord Jesus Christ, it is right for us to remember that the faith and love in our hearts are more important than a location. A baptismal pool in a church on the plains of Texas or the mountains of Colorado, in a village in Mississippi or a great city thronged with people—each can become a place where the believer testifies to his faith in the death and resurrection of Jesus by following him through the waters of baptism.

ILLUSTRATOR PHOTO/KEN TOUCHTON

The Wilderness of Jesus' Temptation

A. Stuart Arnold

"Then was Jesus led up of the Spirit into the wilderness to be tempted of the devil" (Matt. 4:1). Immediately after his baptism Jesus entered the solitude of the wilderness in order to appraise his call and purposes. The alternatives that lay before him had to be faced alone. The Bible gives no positive indication of the wilderness location where Jesus spent those forty days. However, we do have a few clues to help us locate the area. We know that the site must have been fairly near the river Jordan where he was baptized, and we know that it probably was a hilly location from which he could get a view of extensive lands.

Such desert areas are abundant near the river. Jesus easily could have crossed the Jordan to its eastern side. This desert land is crossed today by the road to Amman, capital of the Hashimite Kingdom of Jordan. Bedouins still camp on the flatlands. The plain between the mountains of Judea and the hills of Moab is about twelve miles wide at this point. Beyond the plain the mountains rise and give a spectacular view to the west. There is no valid reason why the temptation could not have taken place in this area. The argument that the ministry of Jesus was centered around the Galilee area and that this district could have been reached more from the wilderness above Jericho does not rule out the Transjordan area. The extra distance is so slight that it would have been only slightly more difficult to travel from it to the north. But very few scholars seriously contend that this was the area. Tradition is unanimously in favor of the wilderness area between the river Jordan and Jerusalem (see photo 7, p. 70).

ILLUSTRATOR PHOTO/KEN TOUCHTON

These hills of the Judean wilderness can be seen in a splendid panorama from the hills of Moab east across the river Jordan. The hills of Judea rise to the west and north. Those nearer to the river have crests that do not rise above sea level, even though they are many hundreds of feet above the river valley. The hills on the western horizon are the tops of the mountains around Jerusalem, including the Mount of Olives. When Moses looked in this direction

Traditional wilderness of Jesus' temptation. Square structure at top left may be part of a Byzantine church. Monasteries were built into the sheer cliffs to commemorate the site (see pp. 46-47).

from Mount Nebo, he must have wondered how such a desert country could ever be called a land flowing with milk and honey. From a distance the hills appear barren, their great round yellow shoulders lying dead under the sun. Is this the place where Jesus faced those issues that shaped his ministry? Tradition says it is.

The visitor may easily get a closer view of the terrain as he drives from Jerusalem to Jericho along the modern road. This road snakes its way down to Jericho, sometimes between hills that press the road into narrow, steep-sided valleys and sometimes over the flatter areas of the round tops of the hills. For a distance of about twelve miles the land drops from 2,723 feet *above* sea level at the Mount of Olives to 1,292 feet below sea level at the Dead Sea. The road leaves Jerusalem to cross the end of the Kidron Valley and then winds around and over the Mount of Olives to the eastern side where it passes through the village of Bethany. Here the land is fertile and olive trees abound. But soon only an occasional tree is seen, and a short distance later even grass and weeds disappear. Across the terrain the scars of trenches dug during the Allenby campaign of World War I remind the visitor that through the centuries this land has seen the strife of conflicts.

To feel the ultimate loneliness that Jesus experienced in his conflict with temptation, one must leave the frequently-traveled road behind. The ancient Roman road, along which the legions marched to beseige the fortress of Masada, passes through the wilderness to the north of the paved highway. The Romans tried to build their roads as straight as a ruler no matter what the nature of the land was that was being crossed. In the Judean wilderness their road is compelled to wind and turn, rise and dip, as it follows the impossible contours of the hills that roll endlessly into the distance. The ground, composed of marl, is a pale yellow.

This place appears completely dead. Not only is the earth barren but also the intense heat becomes hotter and more oppressive as the land drops below sea level. No sound is heard except that of the ever-present insects. The sun stands overhead; there is no shade. Nothing moves on the landscape. Desolation and loneliness leave a man only with himself and the devil—or God.

That lunar-like landscape must be as inhospitable as any place on earth. In this barren wilderness Jesus faced the question as to what God's will meant for him and the world. Entirely cut off from any distractions, he spent forty days alone in this dreadful terrain. No seed grew; no sheep fed. Whose world was it? Why not use miraculous powers to transform into bread one

ILLUSTRATOR PHOTO/KEN TOUCHTON

of the flat, round stones lying on the ground? The absence of any food supply must have made this temptation particularly powerful to the humanity of Jesus, as for six long weeks he considered how he could best use his divine powers.

Nearer to the river and above Jericho the edge of the wilderness is marked by steep-sided hills. One of them is known as Quarantana. It shows an almost perpendicular face to the plain around Jericho. Its name probably was chosen by the Crusaders to commemorate the forty days. In their time a monastery, now ruined, was built on the top of this mountain. From this hill is a magnificent view. The kingdoms of the world were represented below as Jesus saw the scene. Moab, then called Arabia, lay across the Jordan and stretched to the southeast, with its rock-hewn capital at Petra. Jericho, verdant in the valley below, was watered by an aqueduct from Jerusalem and by water from the Wadi Kelt (a wadi is a creek bed, often dry). This was a glorious city as Jesus saw it. Herod the Great,

Quarantania (meaning forty, for 40 days) Monastery, traditional site of first temptation.

king of Judea and friend of Rome, had it built as a winter palace and garden. "The devil . . . sheweth him all the kingdoms of the world, and the glory of them; and saith unto him, All these things will I give thee" (Matt. 4:8-9). From that wilderness, Jesus saw all the kingdoms of the world.

Centuries ago Greek Orthodox monks quarried a monastery into the face of the mountain so that they might share the solitude of the wilderness and be reminded of the trials of the Lord Jesus. Some of the rooms were carved out of the cliff face and so have walls, floor, and ceiling of rock. Other rooms built of masonry cling to the steep slopes. The furniture was sparse—a simple table, a chair or two, possibly an old print of a religious picture hanging on the wall. In past days when the Eastern Orthodox Church was stronger and included the Russian Orthodox Church with its riches and power, the monastery overflowed with monks. Many of them lived in the caves that pock the face of the mountain. Today only a handful of monks continue their service in this forbidding place. Some of the ancient rooms have fragile wooden balconies that hang precariously over drops of several hundred feet. Did the steepness of these hillsides and precipices remind Jesus of that steep hillside where, in Jerusalem, the walls of the Temple towered nearly two hundred feet above the bottom of the Kidron Valley? "Cast thyself down: for it is written, He shall give his angels charge concerning thee: and in their hands they shall bear thee up, lest at any time thou dash thy foot against a stone" (Matt. 4:6).

Jesus knew the hostility of this wilderness and faced its temptations. Out of it he brought a story of tender love that has refreshed, renewed, and revived men and women through the ages.

Christ Tempted

William H. Stephens

Alone. All alone. Alone. Alone.
In barren land of sand and stone
And choking, strangling dust wind-blown
'Round hills that rise up bone on bone
In barren, shrubless demon's home,
He came alone to win his own.

From cooling Jordan waters thrown
By Spirit urge, his task to hone
Messiah's way. His soul lay prone
With hunger's groan and anguish'd moan.
For forty days he fought alone.

Evade. Just evade. Evade. Evade.
"The man you made is justly paid;
He made his life of dismal grade.
Why suffer you? Why be afraid?
Why hunger so?" the Tempter brayed.
Yet bray came soft, 'mid accolade.

"The God you are," the Tempter bade.
A careful, cunning hand he played.
"These stones your might can turn to bread,
Your pangs of hunger to assuade.
Why fight the sun when there is shade?"

From parchéd lips, and hunger-flayed,
The Master prayed. Then fierce assayed:
"To suffer not with man and maid,
My life to be a cheap charade—
I'll live like those I came to aid."

Assure. To assure. Assure. Assure.
Then flashed 'cross sky the world's allure.
"Why take a chance? Just to insure

Opposite: The southeast corner of the Temple Mount is traditionally the Pinnacle of the Temple. In Jesus' day, the building here rose above the wall and the valley was much deeper, making a precipitous distance.

You do not fail, your goal procure,
Give me your hand." With great demur
Again came Tempter's overture.

With might of arms, ambition's cure,
To capture all of kingdoms' lure
And raise the patriot's passion sure
To swift fulfill a cause obscure—
What matters how that end secure?

It matters much, if cause endure.
A man to know a life mature
Ambitions crude he must abjure
And soul commit from motives pure.
Though hard the task, the end is sure.

Amend. So amend. Amend. Amend.
"If you be God, your role defend.
From lofty pinnacle descend.
When angels to your plunge attend,
As Scripture saith, this sign portend
Messiah truly God did send."

Across the sky some sign be penned
So every man may apprehend;
And nevermore shall he contend
With doubt. His soul will mend
As e'er to God his knee shall bend.

ILLUSTRATOR PHOTO/DAVID ROGERS

But men will ever proof rescind,
As fast forgot as is the wind;
On blazing sign men ne'er depend.
The way of faith such proofs transcend;
The way of faith: to call God friend.

Attain. Now attain. Attain. Attain.
The Tempter fled, his work in vain.
'Cross hill and plain a new refrain:
To vict'ry gain o'er irons of Cain
He felt life's strain, ne'er did disdain
To walk with men to share their pain.

Yet Tempter dogged the Master's train
'Til insane crowds asked he be slain;
But grip of grave could not contain.
He broke death's bane, e'er to remain
In heav'n and heart. He did attain.

Jesus, having faced the massive temptations with victory, returned to the region where John was baptizing. When John saw his cousin, he announced that God had revealed to him at Jesus' baptism that this One was the Messiah. Some of John's disciples then left the great prophet-forerunner and became followers of Jesus. Later, they would be called to leave their nets and follow him on a full-time basis.

Evidence that they made the right decision came soon, at a wedding feast in Cana, near Nazareth in Galilee. We do not know where Cana was located. Two sites claim the distinction. Kafr Kanna is accessible to tourists and boasts the church building, but the more likely site is Khirbet Qàna, about nine miles north of Nazareth.

The early weeks and months of Jesus' ministry are somewhat obscure since the Gospels concentrate on his ministry after John was imprisoned. In the meantime, Jesus' following grew rapidly until he "was making . . . more disciples than John" (John 4:1, RSV). This fact aroused opposition among the religious leaders, who were centered in Jerusalem, so Jesus shifted his ministry to Galilee. This trip was the one on which Jesus witnessed to the woman at the well in Sychar.

Jacob's Well

C. Ray Burchette, Jr.

Our Lord was always alert to nature and the world around him. He often used what he saw to teach his followers spiritual truths. We are not surprised, then, that while sitting by Jacob's Well he would use the water illustration to teach a Samaritan woman about the availability of living water which would enable a person never to thirst again (John 4:1-30).

No apparent controversy exists concerning the location of Jacob's Well. The well is not mentioned in the Old Testament, and aside from tradition no evidence exists that it was dug by Jacob or dates from the time of Jacob "who gave us the well" (John 4:12, RSV). However, a tradition going as far back as the time of the Bordeaux Pilgrim, who traveled in Palestine in AD 333, identifies the present location, and no other site competes for the distinction. Jews, Samaritans, Moslems, and Christians are agreed in the identification of Jacob's Well as *Bir Yaqub*.

Returning from Paddanaram, Jacob came to Shechem and pitched his tent east of the city. He purchased that land (Gen. 33:19) located at the mouth of the valley between Mount Ebal and Mount Gerizim, about two miles from Nablus. The well is located at a road junction just north of where the roads from Jerusalem and the Jordan valley join. It is a little over half a mile from Askar, which some scholars accept as Sychar. Sychar may have been a smaller village built on the ruins of Shechem, however, which is closer to the well. Joseph's tomb was on the other side of the ruins.

A number of springs exist in this area, and one might ask why Jacob would go to the trouble of digging a well. He may have had a number of possible reasons. In the East, the law was strict regarding water rights, especially when large herds were concerned. It is possible that when Jacob purchased his land it did not adequately provide for his needs. A well perhaps was needed so as to provide adequate water, give him a measure of independence, and make peace more certain since it would cut down on the possibility of strife between rival herdsmen.

For many years the mouth of the well was unprotected; a fifteen-foot vaulted chamber, whose roof had fallen down, was built over it. In *Recovery of Jerusalem,* Major Anderson tells of a descent made into the well in 1866:

> The mouth of the well has a narrow opening, just wide enough to allow the body of a man to pass through with arms uplifted, and this narrow neck, which is about four feet long, opens into the well itself, which is cylindrically shaped, and about seven feet, six inches in diameter. The mouth and upper part of the well is built of masonry, and the well appears to have been sunk through a mixture of alluvial soil and limestone fragments, till a compact bed of mountain limestone was reached, having horizontal strata which could easily be worked; and the interior of the well presents the appearance of having been lined throughout with rough masonry.

There have been various estimates as to the depth of the well. Arculfus (670) gave the depth as 240 feet. Maundrell (1697) put it at 105 feet. Major Anderson found it to be 75 feet. Originally it must have been deeper than 75 feet. The Samaritan woman told Jesus that the well was "deep" (John 4:11).

From the writings of numerous pilgrims we know that at different times churches have been built over the well. The first, a church built in the form of a cross was constructed sometime in the fourth century with the well at the cross point. There are also remains from a Crusader church that possibly was destroyed by Moslems after their terrible defeat of the Crusaders in 1187. The destruction of these buildings could account for much of the rubbish that has filled the well. Also, travelers had the habit of dropping stones into the well to see how long it took the stone to reach the bottom and so judge the depth of the well.

For all of this, water can still be secured from the well each year until the month of May, sometimes longer. Then it is empty until the rainy season begins. The water might last longer if the well were adequately cleaned. In 1697 Maundrell found fifteen feet of water in the well in May. There is some difference of opinion as to the sources of the water in the well. Some feel that it is fed by water that filters in through the sides, so that it can be considered a spring. Others believe the well depends entirely on the rainfall and percolation. Both processes may be true.

Today the well is owned by the Greek Orthodox Church. When they acquired the land, they built a stone wall, planted the area as an orchard, and provided a keeper. Today an unfinished church, begun in 1903, surrounds the well. To visit the well you descend a stairway that leads below ground into what is left of a crypt of the Crusader church.

Present-day inhabitants of Nablus are much fonder of the "light" water of Jacob's Well that they are of the "heavy" or "hard" water of the neighboring springs. If the same were true in Jesus' day, it would help explain why the Samaritan woman preferred water from the well to any from the springs that might have been closer to her home. But today, even as when Jesus spoke with the Samaritan woman, Jacob's Well provides a water that relieves thirst only for a short time (John 4:13). Only the Christ provides living water.

ILLUSTRATOR PHOTOS/KEN TOUCHTON

Mt. Gerizim rises above the ruins of ancient Shechem. The sacred stone, highlighted in circle at right, likely is from the House of Baal-berith mentioned in Judges 9:4,46.

Mount Gerizim

James A. Brooks

Gerizim, located in central Samaria, rises 2,890 feet above sea level. Mount Ebal is just to the north (3,083 feet). Between the two and about 1,000 feet below their peaks runs a pass that provided the main east-west route across Samaria. Just to the east of these mountains ran the main north-south route through Samaria.

Shechem, mentioned some forty times in the Old Testament, lay at the east end of the pass. We know this ancient city primarily in connection with Jacob, Joseph and his brothers, Joshua, the judges, and the kings Rehoboam and Jeroboam. The strategic importance of Mount Gerizim, Mount Ebal, and Shechem in connection with the pass and the highway intersection is evident.

Mount Gerizim is mentioned by name only four times in the Bible and is alluded to in one other instance. Deuteronomy 11:29-30 and 27:11-13 record Moses' instructions to the Israelites. When they entered the Promised Land they were to march through the pass and observe a solemn ceremony.

Representatives of six of the tribes stood on Mount Gerizim and read a list of blessings that would result from obedience to the covenant, while representatives of the other six tribes stood on Mount Ebal and read a list of curses that would result from disobedience. Joshua 8:30-35 records how these instructions were carried out.

Judges 9:7-21 tells how later Jotham, the son of Gideon, stood on Mount Gerizim and shouted a protest to the men of Shechem below about the treachery of his brother Abimelech. Today a ledge about halfway up the mountain is popularly known as "Jotham's pulpit."

John 4 records the encounter of Jesus and the Samaritan woman. Mount Gerizim is not mentioned by name, but it obviously is referred to in verses 19-21:

Interior of the Tomb of Joseph, near Mt. Gerizim.

The woman said to him . . . , 'Our fathers worshiped on this mountain; and you say that in Jerusalem is the place where men ought to worship.' Jesus said to her, 'Woman, believe me, the hour is coming when neither on this mountain nor in Jerusalem will you worship the Father' (RSV).

In order to understand this passage, one must know something about the Samaritans and their association with Mount Gerizim.

Sometime after the Samaritans emerged as a distinct sect they built a temple on Mount Gerizim. The exact date is uncertain. The Jewish historian Josephus, who wrote late in the first century AD, placed it about 300 BC. Shortly after that date, Alexander the Great conquered Palestine. According to Josephus, the brother of the Jewish high priest had married the daughter of Sanballat, the governor of Samaria. The high priest demanded that his brother divorce this foreigner or be expelled from the priesthood. Sanballat, however, promised to build his son-in-law a temple on Mount Gerizim if he would maintain the marriage. Until recently most scholars doubted the accuracy of Josephus' account. First of all, it appeared that Josephus had confused both the facts and the date of what is recorded in Nehemiah 13:28. Secondly, it was assumed that the Samaritan sect originated in the sixth and fifth centuries BC and that their temple probably was built at that time. Scholarly opinion recently has shifted to a fourth-century date for the origin of Samaritanism. Therefore Josephus' date, if not his account of the circumstances, might be correct after all.

Why did the Samaritans choose Mount Gerizim as the site for their temple? In Samaritan tradition Mount Gerizim is the center of the earth, the most sacred place in the world. The Samaritans believe that Adam was made from its soil and that Abel built the altar (Gen. 4:4) there. They also claim that Noah sacrificed there after the Flood (Gen. 8:20), that it is the land of Moriah where Abraham went to sacrifice Isaac (Gen. 22:2), and that it is the site of Luz or Bethel where Jacob had his dream and later returned to worship God (Gen. 28:11-17; 35:1-7). The Samaritans insist that it is Mount Gerizim rather than Jerusalem where God chose to place his name and to authorize sacrificial worship (Deut. 12:5,11). They further believe that Joshua actually built a temple there (Josh. 24:26; compare Deut. 27:4, which in the Samaritan version reads "Mt. Gerizim" rather than "Mt. Ebal"). Whether all of these traditions existed before the building of the temple on Mount Gerizim is uncertain. They do, however, explain the Samaritan reverence for the mountain.

As long as Palestine was subject to foreign powers the Samaritans and their temple were safe. In 142 BC however, the Jews won their independence, which they were able to main-

Samaritans today still worship on Mt. Gerizim. The high priest lifts the Samaritan scroll high above his head.

tain until the Romans took control in 63 BC. Probably in 128 BC the Samaritan temple was destroyed by the Jewish priest-king John Hyrcanus. With this background it is possible to understand the significance of the Samaritan woman's statement, "Our fathers worshiped on this mountain" (John 4:20, RSV).

Although there no longer was a temple there, it is probable that the Samaritans continued to worship informally on Mount Gerizim during the first Christian century. At least Josephus records how in AD 36 the Roman procurator Pontius Pilate slew some Samaritans who had gathered there to witness the recovery of some objects allegedly hidden by Moses. Josephus also tells about the slaughter of several thousand Samaritans on Mount Gerizim by the Roman general Cerealis during the quelling of the Jewish revolt of AD 66-73, which ironically the Samaritans did not support. Even today, the small group of Samaritans whose synagogue is in modern Nablus still worships on the mountain. Three times each year—at the Feasts of Passover, Pentecost, and Tabernacles—the Samaritans climb their sacred mountain to appear before the Lord. At Passover they camp for a week just west of the summit.

In addition to various surface surveys, there have been three areas of excavation on Mount Gerizim. The first is on the lower north slope, only 350 yards south of ancient Shechem. There a Canaanite temple (seventeenth-sixteenth centuries BC) was uncovered. Second, on the central and highest peak of the mountain two Christian churches have been excavated. One was built by the Byzantine emperor Zeno in the fifth century, the other by the Byzantine emperor Justinian in the sixth century. Third, on a northern spur directly south of the main peak and immediately above the site of ancient Shechem, two temples, one built on top of the remains of the other, have been unearthed. The upper one certainly is the temple of Zeus built by the Roman emperor Hadrian about AD 135. It was approached by a monumental stairway with perhaps 1,500 steps extending the entire length of the slope to the valley floor. The lower temple has not been identified with certainty, but it is highly probable that it represents the remains of the Samaritan temple.

LIBRARY OF CONGRESS/MATSON COLLECTION

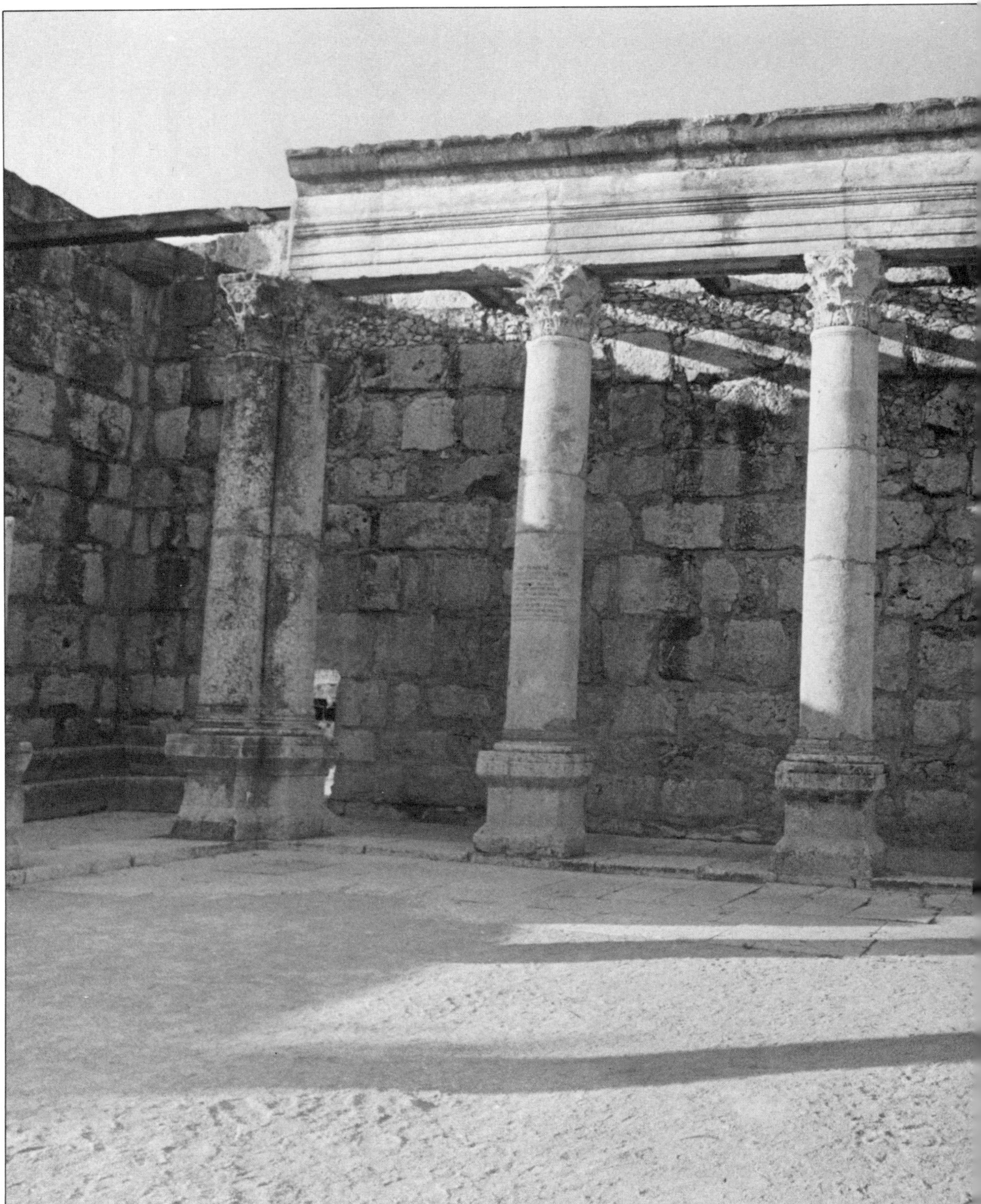

ILLUSTRATOR PHOTO/KEN TOUCHTON

Capernaum

Jack Finegan

In the time of the Gospels, Capernaum was an important town on the Sea of Galilee. Over the course of centuries the town disappeared from sight so completely that now even its location is uncertain.

Clues to the site of ancient Capernaum are provided in the itineraries left by Christian pilgrims who visited the Sea of Galilee during the first few centuries AD. Memories of Gospel events and places evidently were still well-preserved then. Some of these pilgrims were: Aetheria, a nun from the north of Spain or the south of France, who came in AD 385; Theodosius, a visitor known only from his itinerary, who arrived in AD 530; and the Anonymous of Piacenza, a traveler from a city of this name in Italy, who visited in AD 570. Theodosius provides the most detailed sequence of visited places. He traveled from the south by way of Scythopolis and went around the west shore of the lake. He visited in succession Tiberias, Magdala, Seven Springs, and Capernaum. Tiberias is still a large town today, while Magdala is a small village called Migdal. Seven Springs was called *Heptapegon* in Greek. The word became *Tabgha* in Arabic, still a well-known site of springs on the lakeshore. So we know that Capernaum lay yet farther north along the shore.

The Capernaum synagogue, partially restored, dates from the third century AD but apparently was built on earlier foundations. It likely was the site of the synagogue of Jesus' day.

Another clue is in Josephus' autobiography. He writes of being injured one day when thrown from his horse. The accident occurred at the north end of the Sea of Galilee near where the Jordan River flows into the lake. He was carried for help to Capernaum, which must have been the nearest place assistance could be obtained.

The place on the lakeshore between Tabgha to the south and the Jordan to the north where there exist obviously important ruins has long been called Tell Hum. The fact that the name has survived through the centuries is an additional important clue to the site of Capernaum. If the Greek name *Capernaum* came from the Hebrew *Kefar Nahum,* meaning "the village of Nahum," then we would have the name Tell Hum. When the village no longer existed but had deteriorated to a ruin *(tell),* Nahum was shortened to Hum.

ILLUSTRATOR PHOTO/DAVID ROGERS

Capernaum sits on a slope on the northwest shore of the Sea of Galilee.

Edward Robinson, a Bible professor from the United States, traveled in Palestine in 1838 and identified a great many biblical sites which long had been lost. He recognized that the chief ruins at Tell Hum were those of a synagogue. Surprisingly enough, he did not think the place was Capernaum. In 1865, however, the British archeologist Charles Wilson came, concluded that the site was Capernaum, and made the first excavations. In 1894 the Franciscans acquired the site for their Custody of the Holy Land and built a monastery there. With conditions under Turkish rule unsettled, they covered the ruins and planted the field to keep the archeological site safe for the future. In 1905 Heinrich Kohl and Carl Watzinger excavated the synagogue for the *Deutsche Orient-Gesellschaft* and in 1916 published their findings in their *Antike Synagogen in Galilaea.* After that the Franciscans continued the work, under the direction of Brother Wendelin Hinterkeuser in 1905-1914, and in 1921 and afterward under Father Gaudence Orfali. Orfali published his *Capharnaum et ses ruines* in 1922. In 1925 he partially rebuilt the synagogue from its old stones, but his effort was interrupted in 1926 when he was killed in a road accident. In 1953-1954, K. E. W. Wilken reported a small excavation in *Biblisches Erleben im Heiligen Land* (I, p. 214), and in 1970 V. Corbo, S. Loffreda, and A. Spijkerman published their findings of the preceding year in *La Sinagoga di Carfarnao dopo gli scavi del 1969.*

Orfali thought the extant ruins of the synagogue to be from the first century and prior to AD 70. Kohl and Watzinger, however, thought that the synagogues throughout Palestine were destroyed in the Jewish wars against the Romans in AD 70 and 135, and that the present ruins were from a rebuilding of the synagogue at the end of the second or beginning of the third century, as was the case with similar synagogues at Chorazin, Kefar Biram, and other places. Wilken thought that "the foundations of the synagogue undoubtedly belong to the time of Jesus." Father Virgilio Corbo and his associates found a hoard of coins dating to the second half of the fourth century. On that basis they dated the synagogue in the late fourth or

Left: A millstone, made of basalt, with holes for beams, found at Capernaum. *Below:* A third-century AD bas-relief of the ark of the covenant, the oldest representation yet found.

early fifth century. G. Foerster (*Israel Exploration Journal* 21 [1971], pp. 207-209), however, holds that the coins could be the result of repairs and renovations, and that historical and architectural considerations still point to the late second or early third century date. This writer thinks the last opinion the most likely and also would emphasize the persistence of tradition in the rebuilding of synagogues, which makes it probable that the present ruins are on the very site of the synagogue in which Jesus taught.

When Aetheria visited Capernaum she wrote: "There is the synagogue in which the Lord healed the demoniac. One goes up to it by many steps. This synagogue is built of quadrangular stones." The ruins, about one hundred yards from the lakeshore, face south toward Jerusalem. In front there is a raised platform approached by steps leading up from the right, presumably the very steps mentioned by Aetheria. Three doors gave access to the interior, which was a basilica-type hall with rows of columns. Benches ran around three sides. In addition there was a second-story gallery and on the east side a colonnaded court. On one synagogue column a Greek inscription records that it was erected by a certain man named Herod and his children; another column has an Aramaic inscription stating that it was made by Halfu, which is a name corresponding to Alphaeus in Greek (see Mark 2:14). The columns were topped with Corinthian capitals. The sculptured decorations of the synagogue include representations of the ark on wheels, the menorah or seven-armed lampstand, the shofar or ram's horn blown at festivals, the incense shovel, the shield of David, the star of Solomon, and the palm tree (the symbol of the land of Israel). All in all, it was a very handsome building.

At some distance in front of the synagogue toward the lake an octagon of stonework, with a fragment of mosaic, was uncovered in earlier excavations but simply left in place and not identified. One suggestion was that it had been part of a fountain in a public square in front of the synagogue. Investigation of this octagon and the surrounding area was included in the work done at Capernaum by Virgilio Corbo and his associates in 1969. Father Corbo reported his findings in a preliminary report in 1969 and a final report in 1972, each under the title, *The House of St. Peter at Capernaum.*

ILLUSTRATOR PHOTO/KEN TOUCHTON

Above and opposite, top: Remains of homes between the synagogue and the so-called house of Peter, with walls and cobblestone floors.

In the entire excavated area the remains of many habitations have been uncovered. These are houses generally built of large black basalt stones gathered from the shore of the lake or the surrounding fields. The large stones were laid dry without any mortar and the interstices (spaces between) were closed with smaller stones. The stones were dressed or worked only for the sills and door jambs. The floors were of black basalt stones that rest on the earth. The roofs probably were of wooden beams covered with a mixture of earth and straw, the very kind of roof in which an opening was made through which the paralytic was lowered (Mark 2:4). In various houses were found Herodian pottery, Herodian lamps, coins of Herod Agrippa I (AD 41-44) and the procurators, and coins of the first Jewish revolt. The place, therefore, was occupied from the first century and onward, and so we have a glimpse of a modest section of the town of that time.

In the center of the area just described is the octagon and directly under it, Corbo found a hall which was constructed originally as a habitation just like all the others. But this particular room received special treatment. The floor was repeatedly paved with lime, the walls were plastered, and the plaster was decorated with pictures and graffiti (wall writings) in Greek, Hebrew, and Syriac. This half probably was enlarged in the fourth century by taking in neighboring rooms, and the whole precinct was surrounded by a wall. The particular room just described still was in the center. The coins and pottery found extend from the first to the fifth century, and there fragments of cooking pots, pans, jars, lamps, and even two fishhooks also were found.

Evidently an ordinary house in the fishing village of Capernaum was considered worthy of special respect. The graffiti have been published by E. Testa, *I Graffiti della Casa di S. Pietro* (1972). Almost all of the markings come from the main hall. The inscriptions contain parts of prayers (such as "have mercy" and "amen"), names (including the name "of Peter" and an invocation to Christ the Lord, "Lord Jesus Christ help"). The pictures are symbols, such as the

Below: A succession of octagon buildings over the site celebrated as early as the fourth century as Peter's house. The age of the tradition is impressive.

coat and the cross, otherwise known to have been used by the Jewish Christians, as Testa has shown in his *Il simbolismo dei Giudeo-Cristiani* (1962).

It was exactly over this obviously venerated half that the octagonal structure later was built. It consisted, as we know now, of two concentric octagons and a portico on five sides, with mosaic floors, and—added later—an apse on the east side, a baptistery, and some side rooms. The mosaics include rosettes, flowers, and a peacock, the symbol of immortality. The mosaics are similar in execution to those at Tabgha, believed to belong to the end of the fourth or beginning of the fifth century. Here also the coins associated with the octagon do not extend beyond the end of the fourth and the beginning of the fifth century. Therefore, we

The spiral pattern was common during the period of the Capernaum synagogue, such as on these false columns.

ILLUSTRATOR PHOTO/KEN TOUCHTON

conclude that the octagon was a Byzantine church belonging to the middle of the fifth century. (The Byzantine Empire grew out of the Roman Empire's eastern capital at Constantinople.)

In his itinerary, the pilgrim called the Anonymous of Piacenza reports: "We came to Capernaum into the house of St. Peter, which is a basilica." Presumably this reference is to the Byzantine church built in the preceding century and just described. In her itinerary, Aetheria says: "In Capernaum out of the house of the first of the apostles a church was made, the walls of which stand until today as they once were. Here the Lord cured the paralytic." This reference well can refer to the house church, as we have described it above, since it stood in the fourth century.

The resulting conclusions are summarized by Corbo: (1) In the entire area a complex of habitations of the first century has been found. (2) In this complex one house was venerated in a special way from the first century onward by the local community of Jewish Christians. (3) In about the fourth century this house was enlarged by adding dependencies and the whole was enclosed within a sacred precinct. (4) The belief of the Jewish Christians in Capernaum and of the pilgrims as to the special character of the place—indicated by tradition as the house of the apostle Peter—is expressed in the inscriptions and symbols on the walls of the venerated hall. (5) In about the middle of the fifth century a church with a plan of two concentric octagons, a portico on five sides, and subordinate rooms on other sides, was constructed over the house.

To G. Foerster (*Israel Exploration Journal* 21 [1971], p. 211) these conclusions seem "conceivable, but not proven"; and the *Bulletin of the American School of Oriental Research* (No. 212, Dec., 1973, p. 34) advises that the conclusions should be read "with caution." To this writer, however, the evidence seems impressive and quite in accord with many other recent findings which show that the early Christians in the Holy Land had a lively remembrance of many places which were associated with Jesus and therefore were important to them.

Bethsaida

C. Ray Burchette, Jr.

Just where was the city of Bethsaida located? Were there two cities with the same name? Was one of those cities in Galilee? Were Bethsaida and Julias the same city or different ones? The answers are silent secrets known only by the years.

Bethsaida, which most likely means "house of the fisher," played a small but significant part in the life of Jesus and his disciples. It is referred to as the birthplace of Philip, Andrew, and Peter (John 1:44; 12:21; although Peter had a house in Capernaum, Matt. 8:14). At Bethsaida Jesus healed a blind man (Mark 8:22). Bethsaida was near the place where Jesus fed five thousand persons (Mark 6:45), and Jesus went there when he learned of the death of John the Baptist (Luke 9:10). Jesus' ministry evidently was not well received in Bethsaida, and the town received strong condemnation from Jesus (Matt. 11:21).

Philip the Tetrarch, son of Herod the Great, raised the town to the status of a city and named it Julias in honor of the daughter of Augustus. Since Julia fell from favor and was banished in 2 BC the foundation of the city must have been laid prior to that time. Philip was buried in Bethsaida.

Many feel that Bethsaida and Julias were two close but separate cities. The older fishing village was located on the shore of the Sea of Galilee and identified with an area known as Khirbet el-'Araj. El-'Araj boasts a natural harbor, which until recent times was used by fishermen from Tiberias. A site east of the Jordan, *et-Tell*, about two miles from the sea, is identified as Julias. It contains remains of a city wall and an ancient mosaic. A Roman road and traces of an aqueduct connect the two cities.

Were there at one time two cities named Bethsaida? A statement in John's Gospel raises that question. John wrote that Philip was from "Bethsaida of Galilee" (John 12:21). Most sources indicate that the Jordan formed the

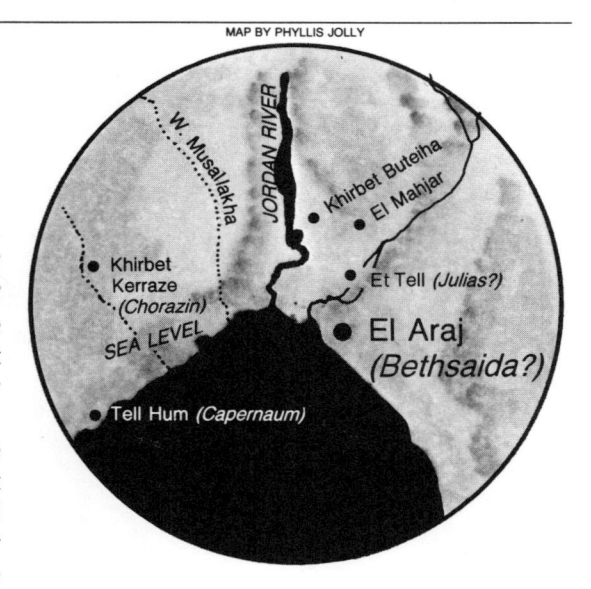

Sea of Galilee, looking from Tiberius toward Mt. Hermon. Bethsaida was located on the north shore, slightly east, in this line of vision.

boundary of Galilee on the east and that Bethsaida-Julias was beyond that boundary. Some writers have attempted to reconcile this verse with other references to Bethsaida by extending the territory of Galilee. Others have opted for two Bethsaidas. Those who opt for a second Bethsaida locate it at *ain et-Tabighah* about three miles southwest of the mouth of the Jordan. It seems improbable that there would have been two cities by the same name so close together. J. S. Thompson (*The Bible and Archeology*) suggests that any city built at the mouth of the narrow Jordan, as Bethsaida-Julias was, necessarily would have some houses or suburbs on the west bank of the river, which would be in Galilee. George Adam Smith does not feel we must hold to the idea of two Bethsaidas. He wrote that the province of Galilee ran around the lake and included most of the level coastland on the east, thus eliminating the necessity of more than one Bethsaida. At any rate, Bethsaida lay so close to the border that it could be considered in the region, if not the technical boundaries, of Galilee.

Our questions about Bethsaida cannot be answered fully at this time. But as you ponder the place and fate of that city once honored by Philip the Tetrarch, you can almost hear the words of Jesus: "Woe unto thee, Bethsaida! for if the mighty works, which were done in you, had been done in Tyre and Sidon, they would have repented long ago in sackcloth and ashes. But I say unto you, It shall be more tolerable for Tyre and Sidon at the day of judgment, than for you" (Matt. 11:21-22).

Left: Herod's summer palace fortress, the Herodium, near Bethlehem. *Above:* Bethlehem seen from the Herodium.

ILLUSTRATOR PHOTO:DAVID ROGERS

Right: The sunsets over Bethlehem are breathtaking, as though God singled out this barren hill city for a special beauty. *Above:* Altar and incense vessels above the traditional spot where Jesus was born.

ILLUSTRATOR PHOTO/KEN TOUCHTON

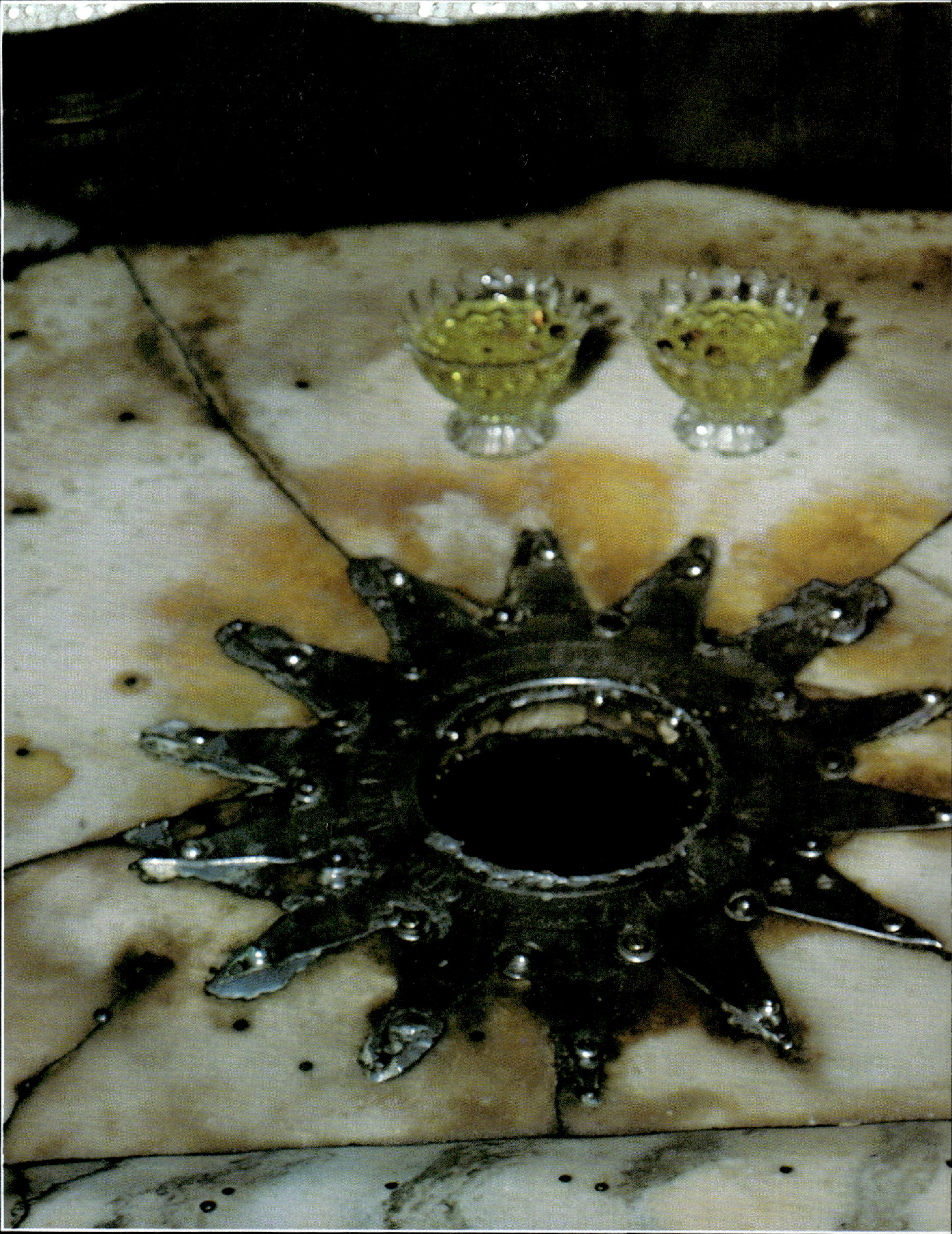

ILLUSTRATOR PHOTO KEN TOUCHTON

ILLUSTRATOR PHOTO DAVID ROGERS

Left: A silver star set in marble marks the spot of Jesus' birth. *Above right:* Road from Jerusalem to Bethany and Jericho beyond ran into the valley and over the arid hills beyond.

ILLUSTRATOR PHOTO/KEN TOUCHTON

BROADMAN FILMS/MURRAY SEVERANCE

Opposite, bottom: The Valley of Megiddo, not far from Nazareth, was a scene of many battles. *Above:* Jezreel, the east side of the Megiddo valley, was on Jesus' route from Nazareth to Jerusalem. *Large photo:* The wilderness of Judea looking from the Herodium toward the Dead Sea. *Opposite, top:* The barren region of rolling hills was part of the traditional wilderness of Jesus' temptation

Below: Upper Jordan River and Mt. Hermon, seen from Hazor in east Galilee. *Right:* The Sea of Galilee, in one of its many moods, looking toward Mt. Hermon. Only rippled now, the lake could become tempestuous.

Above: The Cyrus Cylinder, which tells of Cyrus' policy of restoring exiles to their lands, resulting in Jerusalem's restoration.
Right: Southern Perea, seen from Mt. Nebo.
Bottom right: The columned street of Gerasa, one of the Decapolis.

The Sea of Galilee

William H. Stephens

ILLUSTRATOR PHOTO/KEN TOUCHTON

Tiberius, built by that "old fox" Herod Antipas, commands Sea of Galilee.

People have lived around the Sea of Galilee since long before history was recorded. Lying 696 feet below sea level, summer exists the year around, and today the lake boasts forty species of fish.

The Sea of Galilee is really a lake, and generally it is called a lake in the ancient sources. It is heart-shaped and measures about twelve miles north to south by about five miles east to west. But in spite of its lake size, a large lake, to be sure, the Sea of Galilee is massive in terms of its importance to world history, for it is so closely aligned to the life of Christ.

The earliest name we have for this 200-foot deep body of water is Lake of Chinnereth, so-called after its major ancient town. Chinnereth was a major city from at least the fifteenth century BC (about three centuries before Joshua's conquest) until the end of the Old Testament period. During the Interbiblical Period (the period between the Old and New Testaments) the name was Gennesar, which it also was called during New Testament times along with its more familiar name, Sea of Galilee. A hundred years or so after Christ it became the Sea (or Lake) of Tiberias, named after Herod Antipas' new city on the west shore.

The Sea of Galilee can almost be encircled today by car, with a little luck and good traction. The Jordan River enters the sea on the north between Capernaum and Bethsaida-Julias, the first and last stop on our journey as we drive south along the west side and back north then along the east side (see photo 12, p. 72).

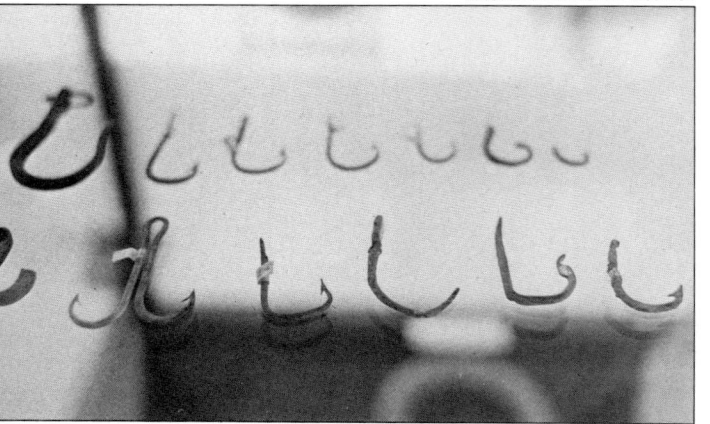

Left: Bronze fishhooks, Roman period. *Above:* Magdala, once a prosperous and important lakeside city on a crossroad to Nazareth.

From Capernaum (see p. 56) at the north end of the Plain of Gennesaret, we drive only one and a quarter miles to Tabgha, the traditional site of the feeding of the five thousand. The place is not authentic, for the Gospels are clear that the miracle took place on the east side of the lake, but a church building was located at Tabgha anyway as early as the fourth century. The area is historic. A hill beside Tabgha is the Mount of the Beatitudes, the traditional site of the Sermon on the Mount. There are also ruins of a church building that has been dated to the fourth century.

Tell el-Oreinah is only a half-mile further south. It likely is the hilltop site of Old Testament Chinnereth. We continue along the shore to Magdala (Migdal, or Mejdel), at the south end of the Plain of Gennesaret. This home of Mary Magdalene reflected Greek (Hellenistic) culture, was famous for its salted fish, which it exported, and had a reputation of gross corruption. Little remains of the town today.

The deep chasm, Wadi el-Haman, flows into the Sea of Galilee just north of Magdala. Many caves, cut into the cliff face and almost inacces-

Modern, bustling Tiberius is the dominant city along the sea. It lies about four miles south of Magdala. Herod Antipas created Tiberias about AD 17-20. He transferred his capital there from Sepphoris but, because the city was built over a graveyard, Jews would not live there. Herod had to bring in foreign settlers. Later, though, in the second century, Tiberius became a Jewish center of learning. About a mile and a quarter south are located the famous hot springs called el-Hammath (Josh. 19:35). The earliest synagogue yet excavated in Galilee is located here.

Lead weights from Sea of Galilee, Roman period, from Kursi east of the lake.

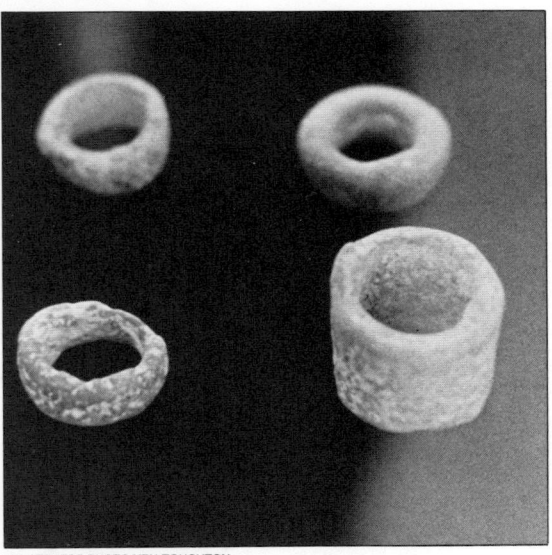

sible, protected rebels from the Roman army, and, earlier, the Maccabees from the Greeks. The important Maccabean city of Arbela is farther up the chasm.

The Horns of Hattin rise southwest of Arbela, a dominant feature among the mountains surrounding the sea. They are the traditional place of the Sermon on the Mount. However, the site is much too far from Capernaum to qualify; in fact, the tradition dates back only some three hundred years. The real significance of Hattin is that here the last-ditch battle took place in which the Crusaders lost control of Palestine to the Moslems, led by Saladin.

South of Tiberius the mountains to the west move in close to the sea until we arrive at a plain at the south end that opens up wide, green, and lush. An ancient Canaanite worship center to the moon was located here at Beth-yerah. This massive site covered sixty acres in its heyday, during the Early Bronze Age, and may have been the dominant city of the region. In fact, during the Stone Age an important culture called the Yarmukian centered in this region and the Yarmuk River that flows into the Jordan a short distance to the south. By the time Joshua entered Cannaan, Beth-yerah was long since

Above: Basalt stone anchor, 1st—2nd centuries AD, found at the Sea of Galilee. *Top:* Southern end of the lake. *Top right:* The high tableland of Bashan and Geshur beyond the lake. *Right:* The lake from the north.

destroyed, possibly by the Hyksos in the seventeenth century BC. It was not occupied again until the Greek-Egyptian ruler Ptolemy II built a city there sometime prior to 218 BC in honor of his sister and named it Philoteria. The Maccabean ruler Alexander Jannaeus destroyed Philoteria in the first century BC.

Circling the south end, we turn north to follow the road along the east side of the sea. The Golan Heights lies sharply to our right. Ein Gev lies on the coastal plain about halfway up the length of the sea. A cone-shaped hill rises behind Ein Gev on which the Decapolis city of Hippos stood. The Aramaeans had a fortress there in the tenth century BC.

Continuing north, we pass some more hot springs before coming to Kursi, some three miles from Ein Gev. This site fits the conditions for the miracle of the demon-possessed man and the swine. Tombs are cut into the rock close by, and a boat can approach the town easily.

Bethsaida-Julias is the last site on our journey around the sea. It has not been identified with certainty but appears to be Khirbet el-Araj (see chapter, "Bethsaida").

One of the most memorable events in a visitor's itinerary today is the sunrise journey from Tiberias to Capernaum by boat. Many guides hold a worship service as the sun breaks over the eastern hills. The sunsets, too, are beautiful, with the reflections of the red mountains to the east. Jesus selected a restful, comfortable place to make his headquarters when he selected Capernaum. But, too, the Sea of Galilee was a busy region, accessible to each direction, and people—whom he came to serve and win—were there in abundance.

The Sermon on the Mount

Matthew presented Jesus as the Messiah who was sent by God to inaugurate the kingdom of God. His purpose is clear not only in his frequent references to prophecies fulfilled in Christ but also in the structural arrangement of the book itself.

The Sermon on the Mount is a key in Matthew's plan (*sermon* is *our* word). Matthew said "He sat down . . . and taught them" (Matt. 5:1-2, RSV). Matthew's purpose was to draw distinct parallels with the giving of the covenant at Mount Sinai. God spoke then from a mountain; he also spoke from a mountain in Christ. God summed up the law in the Ten Commandments then; Jesus summed up his sermon in the Beatitudes. The Ten Commandments later were elaborated into a series of applications; Jesus elaborated the Beatitudes and made applications to life. The same spirit of love and right attitude runs as a thread through both the old and the new covenants.

The Sermon on the Mount has been called the manifesto of the kingdom, for it gives guidelines for living in the kingdom Christ came to establish. The poem "Kingdom Come" seeks to explain the meaning of the Beatitudes and, thus, the Sermon on the Mount.

FOREIGN MISSION BOARD, SBC/FON SCOFIELD

Kingdom Come

William H. Stephens

The Crowd.
An anxious multitude, mosaic throng;
   some talked, some wept, some burst with song.
All raised their eyes to realize
Messiah come.
He's here. Up there. Now soon he'll share

The Words.
The voice of God to men—long silent now—
   we'll hear, we'll know, we'll loud avow.
And we shall follow.

We shall fight; our maids shall weep
   with glistening tears of pride;
Our children dream, and while they sleep
   they'll march the marshaled stride.

From other mount, eons before,
   God's voice 'mid lightning pealed.
On shrouded Sinai's desert floor
   his chosen people kneeled.
A diff'rent place, that barren land,
   from Horns of Hattin's plain.
The crowd closed 'round disciple band
   Messiah's word to gain.

The poor in spirit blessed be.
Ah, poor are we.
The Romans made us so.
Those cursèd Romans.

In grasping lies the loss of life—
    the want, desire, compulsive strife.
To walk away from hideous life.
Ah, the victory!
No more to know the pressure toll,
    the compromise, the captive soul.
No more to fight the mirror's glare
    reflecting morning's anxious stare.
To touch the mystery divine,
To sit with God and taste new wine.
Blessed be the spirit poor.
Their future in God's kingdom sure.

Blessed be the ones who mourn.
Ah, sad are we.
The Romans made us so.
Those cursèd Romans.

No love in hardness finds its nest;
    a life aloof ne'er comfort blessed.
To walk back into hideous life.
Ah, the victory!
To see and weep with kingdom heart,
    to heal the hurt from devil dart.
To leap in maelstrom's heady dross
    with naught to calm but heaven's Cross.
To care, and feel, and love, and long
    to sing to men a better song.
Blessed be the ones who mourn.
My comfort theirs; their lives reborn.

In wonder gazed the restless crowd;
    with smirk and twitch, one spat to ground:
"But fools they are, such men as these!
    a ragtag lot, with cowards' pleas.
Ascetic monks who seek escape,
    do-gooders, starry eyes agape."

The Teacher paused. His sweeping gaze
    brought hush to murm'ring crowd.
Then gently, ever gently raised
    his voice. Then forceful vowed:

The meek be blessed. The earth is theirs.
Each trait inane that stands alone,
    but pressed together, heaven's own.
The man who sees far heaven's door
    is truly free, free at the core.
To walk in peace with God and man.
Ah, the victory!
To fear the Structure's club no more;
    to grieve for naught from earthly store.
With confidence through ev'ry trial,
    to smile in silence all the while.
Self-possessed, within God's might
    formidable. The meek can fight.
The meek be blessed. His soul's rebirth
    an act of God, who owns the earth.

Blessed be the ones who thirst
And hunger long for righteousness.
Ah, we hunger
And thirst—
But to be free!

Anarchy's hand is tempting cruel;
   it swears of ease, but hard its rule.
To drink the dregs of Absolute.
Ah, the victory!
To feel the growl of hunger's gnaw,
   discover then the error's flaw;
To wrestle hard, each muscle strain,
   then taste the cool of honest rain—
A search for life, experience.
A lab, a book, a scholar's sense.
Where cross the line of life and book,
   for righteousness and truth, there look.
Who zealous hungers for God's word
   the truth shall know; he shall be heard.

Blessed are the merciful.
Ah, we want mercy.
From those Romans.
Those cursèd Romans.

At mourning tempers spirit-poor,
   so law with mercy is made truer.
The voice from Sinai thundered hot
   a rulebook life of "Thou shalt not."
The wineskin burst. Now mercy's cruse
   pays not to man what are his dues.
And mercy shown is mercy known.
   So likewise live, God tells his own.
Blessed are the merciful,
For mercy they shall know.

The fidget-fingered crowd, confused,
   more restless grew, and still they mused
Of battle dust and hobnailed noise.
   They smiled, admired Messiah's poise.

Blessed are the pure in heart.
How cursed, that vacillating soul—
   the doubt, despair, the hard truth's stare.
To look at life with paring knife.
Ah, the victory!
To cut away the overlay, stif'ling weeds, the foul decay;
From deep within the heartbeat mind,
   to know the task that men must find—
With heart made pure with white-hot heat,
   with God's own arm on anvil beat.
Blessed be whose hearts are pure.
Their sight of God one day is sure.

Blessed be the peacemakers.
Ah, we want peace! One day it comes
When Romans gone.
Those cursèd Romans.

Shall peace be born, contention's child?
   from womb of war or anger riled?
To find the key to peace on earth.
Ah, the victory!
Peacemaker cloak ne'er worn alone.
   The spirit-poor must also mourn,
And meek must be, and thirst endure,
And mercy give from heart that's pure.
A shortcut peace from shortcut men
   shall never peace on earth extend.

Messiah's peace. A lonely word
   the Christian world has hardly heard.
God's child is he who maketh peace;
Oh him God's blessings never cease.

The persecuted shall be blessed.
For life to count so much, so much.
Ah, the victory!
'Tis yet another blest refrain:
He who would count must count through pain.
Commitment knows no boundary.
The world is one. It must be free.
Disciple, knowing God's embrace
   in life and death, stands in his place.

Not one of those who heard that day
   could understand Messiah's way—
A fellowship of men who care,
   and live, and give, and love, and share.

ILLUSTRATOR PHOTO/KEN TOUCHTON

Nain

By the time Jesus raised from the dead the widow's son at Nain, he was about halfway through his earthly ministry. Since the Gospels deal so heavily with the last half of Jesus' ministry, many of the great teachings, events, and miracles were still to come. Even so, by this time Jesus' fame had spread widely. He had healed many persons, had been rejected at Nazareth, had called his twelve disciples, had toured Galilee, and already had experienced controversy with religious authorities including efforts to have him killed. The raising of the widow's son, then, was an incredible demonstration of divine power and was a clear sign of Jesus' power even over death.

Nain is located between Mounts Gilboa and Tabor, on the lower slope of the Old Testament Hill of Moreh. Today it is the small Arab village of Naim (meaning "pleasant"). Ruins scattered to the north indicate that Nain was occupied both in Old Testament and in Roman times. A small church building of fairly recent date and the ruins of a shrine commemorate the site.

The Sudden Storms of Galilee

Denis Baly

What we would think of as no more than the lake of Galilee, twelve miles long by five miles wide, is almost always called the "Sea" (Greek *thalassa*) in the Bible. Only Luke, a Gentile and a foreigner, calls it a "Lake" (*limne*). For the people of Palestine, therefore, small though it is, the lake represented an upwelling of the Great Deep, the terrifying element of chaos and disorder. Moreover, immediately on the further side lay Gentile territory, in Jewish eyes pagan, corrupt, and possessed of a legion of devils. The account in Mark 4:35 to 5:20 of the storm on the lake and the healing of the Gadarene demoniac demonstrates this view clearly and should be compared with Psalm 65, which Mark no doubt had in mind. That psalm states that God "stilleth the noise of the seas, the noise of their waves, and the tumult of the people. They also that dwell in the uttermost parts are afraid at thy tokens" (vv. 7-8; compare Mark 4:39; 5:15-17).

But just how accurate is Mark's description? Very accurate, indeed; for despite the denials of some critics, it is evident that Mark knew Palestine well. The situation in his day resembled somewhat the period between 1948 and 1967. I remember sitting in Tiberias then on the western side of the lake one Passover festival. I was looking at the dark other side, interrupted only by the lights of the little kibbutz of Ein-Gev. This passage came immediately to my mind. "There," I thought to myself, "is the foreign world. There they do not keep the feast." So it was in the time of the Gospels.

Moreover, anyone familiar with Galilee knew the abrupt and violent storms that rouse the quiet waters to dangerous disorder. This phenomenon is not peculiar to Palestine, but is characteristic of lakes anywhere when they are enclosed within steep mountain slopes. The Lake of Lucerne in Switzerland and the Dead Sea in Palestine itself know such storms well. Those storms are the result of two simple facts: Water retains its warmth longer than the surrounding land, and the warm air above the lake tends to rise whereas cold air sinks. When the sides of the lake are steep, this movement of the air is exaggerated. The cold air pours down the hillsides like a flood, suddenly displacing the warmer air, which is forced upward. The fact that the Rift Valley, which contains both the Lake of Galilee and the Dead Sea, is considerably below sea level naturally means that the air within it normally is very warm.

These invading masses of air may pour down onto the Lake of Galilee from any one of three directions: north, east, and west, whereas southerly winds are themselves warm and move gradually upward toward the lake. Winter winds coming from the north can cause a sudden drop of temperature, for they come from the snow-covered heights of Lebanon and Mount Hermon, but since their rapid descent occurs further north they seldom cause any violent disturbance.

During the two intermediate seasons, between the major seasons of winter and summer, the excessively hot, dry *sirocco* can blow from the east, sometimes for days at a time. It is by no means cold, of course, but it is both a descending mass of air and very powerful. It is also erratic and, though it makes the surface of the lake no more than choppy, sudden gusts can give trouble to the smaller boats.

The more frequent winds come from the west. In the summer months the daily sea breeze takes time to build up over the hills of Galilee and then, early in the afternoon, descends with surprising abruptness to the lake, sweeping through the narrow valleys to the Plain of Gennesaret and down the hillsides to Tiberias, rousing the lake's smooth surface. It is, however, very regular and predictable and the local inhabitants know with remarkable exactness when to expect it.

Very different are the storm winds of winter, which may blow at any time from the beginning of October to the end of April, bringing with them urgently needed rain. They are "mighty winds" accompanying depressions, which at this season pass along the Mediterranean across Palestine toward Iran and the Persian Gulf, and their strength is, of course, increased by the descent. The air is very unstable, and the sudden displacement of the warm lake air by the wet and thrusting westerlies often creates a rapidly rising current of air and dramatic thunderstorms. Though the strong west wind, accompanied as it is by slashing rain, can cause disturbance enough, the swiftly rising column of air in the thunderstorm tends to pull in cooler air from every side, swirling round in a broad and violent counterclockwise movement. This movement can cause sudden shifts of wind direction over the lake, and consequently greater difficulties for the sailor.

As has been said, somewhat similar conditions can prevail over the Dead Sea, further south. There the shoreline is almost 1,300 feet below sea level, the heat consequently greater, and the slopes of either side very much higher and more precipitous. Winds can pour down into the Rift Valley in this region with tremendous force, though once in the valley they are channeled by the towering containing walls in either a northerly or southerly direction. The salt-laden water is so dense that it is not easily disturbed, but once roused the waves can have remarkable strength and toss the boats around like corks.

Perhaps two personal reminiscences may illustrate the kind of thing that can happen. Both occurred during the time of the British Mandate. One winter a small group of us arranged to walk down the narrow gorge of the Jordan from Lake Huleh to the lake of Galilee. When we started it was clear that we were in for a very wet day, but being all British, we took rain for granted and walked resolutely through it. By the time we reached the southern end of the gorge, the wind from the west was approaching gale force and the rain was torrential. The lake was in a tumult and the police launch from Tiberias, which we had arranged to meet us, was unable to make the journey. We were compelled to borrow horses and plod along the waterlogged shore till we reached the Plain of Gennesaret where a car could pick us up.

On another winter day I had gone down to spend a little while at the southern end of the Dead Sea, visiting a family at the potash works, which in those days could be reached only by boat. The journey southward was smooth, but a sudden storm developed while I was on shore and the return journey was exceedingly rough. The tug, which was towing two barges full of men and women returning from their two-week shift at Sedom, had great difficulty in coming alongside the jetty at the northern end of the Sea. All of us were completely drenched by the waves, and the great majority of the passengers were helpless from seasickness.

These sudden and savage storms are, therefore, not a mere traveler's tale, but an undoubted fact.

DENIS BALY

Jesus' Wider Ministry

William H. Stephens

We are used to thinking of Jesus in Galilee and Judea, but he traveled far beyond those boundaries. Tyre and Sidon, well up the Phoenician coast, also were visited by Jesus, whose fame preceded him there.

He made several trips across the Sea of Galilee into the lands ruled by Philip the Tetrarch, a son of Herod the Great. This region fanned out from the northeast shore of the sea to include the desert and marginal regions and also several important cities, including Caesarea Philippi.

Jesus also had a ministry in the Decapolis, a large region dominated by cities patterned after the Greek model. This region fanned out to the east from the southeastern shore of the Sea of Galilee and also included the area around Scythopolis (Old Testament Beth-shean), which lay west of the Jordan.

Perea, also, knew Jesus' ministry. This region included land east of the Jordan and partly surrounded by the Decapolis. It extended to the south about halfway down the Dead Sea and bordered the large Nabatean kingdom, whose capital was the famed red city of Petra.

Caesarea Philippi was the capital of Philip's domain. It lies at the foot of Mount Hermon, at one of the four sources of the Jordan River, very close to Old Testament Dan. These headwaters have been a worship center since time immemorial. During Roman times the principal god was Pan, god of the flocks. Herod built a shrine there to honor Augustus; then Philip named the town after the Caesar—he added his own name to distinguish it from Caesarea on the Mediterranean Sea. Before that the town was called Paneas, from which the current name Banias is derived.

The city was a pagan center and had a well-developed Hellenistic culture; that is, it was planned along the lines of a Greek city, according to an aggressive policy instituted by Alexander the Great, continued by his successors, and then by the Romans. The fact that Titus celebrated the capture of Jerusalem there indicates its importance.

This water source of the Jordan springs from a massive cliff face, making its way today around and through tumbled stones from the collapsed roof of a former cave. Three niches can be seen in the cliff face; they held pagan statues at one time.

The region is one of the most beautiful in the Holy Land, green, pleasant, and well-watered (see photo 11, p. 72). During a visit to some of the villages of the region, Jesus asked the question that brought Peter's Great Confession. Shortly thereafter Peter, James, and John witnessed the transfiguration.

Mount Tabor in Galilee claims to be the site of the transfiguration. Most likely, it was claimed as the place because of its accessibility.

Far left: Mt. Hermon slopes. *Left:* Ancient sacred caves, in Jesus' day dedicated to Pan. *Below:* Headwaters of one Jordan branch. All three sites near Caesarea Philippi.

Mount Hermon is a much better candidate, though, for the event is mentioned along with the visit to Caesarea Philippi. No shrine, building, or local legend claims to identify the spot, which must be somewhere up the steep slopes of this highest mountain in the land.

We cannot know how extensively Jesus traveled in the region of the Decapolis; most likely, he visited only those cities that lay in its western part. Decapolis means "ten cities"; but as time went by the number fluctuated as well as which cities were included. The Decapolis was a federation of Hellenized cities, each independent or quasi-independent. The cities originally were established or reestablished as a system of fortifications to protect either the Seleucids (Greek rulers in Syria) against the Ptolemies (Greek rulers in Egypt) or vice versa. They also served to provide stability against nomads and tribes people and a showcase of Greek culture in "uncultured" areas.

The original Decapolis probably included Raphana, Canatha, Dion, Gadara, Hippos, Pella, Gerasa, Philadelphia, Scythopolis, and Damascus. During the New Testament period Abila was included, while Damascus was at the edge of the Nabatean (Arabia) kingdom. Eight of these cities lay within a reasonably short distance to the Sea of Galilee or the Jordan River. Damascus is some sixty miles northeast of the sea, as the crow flies, while Raphana was about thirty miles east and Canatha about sixty miles east. The Decapolis, not counting Gadara, is mentioned three times in the Gospels: Matthew 4:25; Mark 5:20; 7:31.

Raphana may be ancient Ashtoret, located on Tell Ashtara. Little is known about the city.

Information also is meager regarding Canatha. Some exploration has been done at Qanawat, its location; the present ruins date to the Roman period. Canatha likely became a Hellenized city during the period of Greek domination.

87

Scythopolis, the only Decapolis city west of the Jordan, is ancient Beth-shean. The Old Testament city, which is very ancient, lay on top of a huge mound whose sides slope at a forty-five degree angle. By Roman times the city had spread into the valley. This city dominated the pass from the Valley of Megiddo, through the Jezreel Valley to the Jordan. It was dominated by Egypt from the fifteenth to the thirteenth centuries BC, then gradually became Philistine. It was not conquered during the Conquest and when Saul was killed much later the inhabitants hung his body from the city walls. David subdued the city and Solomon established a garrison there.

ILLUSTRATOR PHOTO/DAVID ROGERS

Ancient Beth-shean, called Scythopolis in Jesus' day, was the only Decapolis city west of the Jordan.

By New Testament times Scythopolis extended in a wide area beyond the tell. This Roman theater lay in the valley.

The city declined under the Persians, then the Greeks changed its name to Scythopolis, a name some ancient writers thought came from the Scythians' invasion of Palestine. If the name came from the Scythians, more likely the reason was that a garrison of Scythian mercenaries were stationed there. At any rate, the city was Gentile in Jesus' day; we have no indication that he went there. Later, Armenian Christians dominated, and the city became an important bishopric seat. Ruins of several church buildings exist there. The ancient name of Beth-shean was restored by the Arabs when they conquered Palestine.

Four Decapolis cities are grouped fairly close to the Sea of Galilee: Hippos, Dion, Abila, and Gadara. Dion is the farthest. Two sites are candidates for its location, each on opposite sides of a chasm: Tell el-Husn and Tell el-Ash'ari. Dion dates back at least to about 3000 BC (if it is Tel el-Husn). It was established as a Macedonian (Greek) colony. Alexander Jannaeus (103-76 BC), the Maccabean king, captured the city as he did several of its companions. The Roman general Pompey granted Dion self-government. El-Husn has produced considerable Roman and Byzantine evidence.

Hippos is Susita; both words mean horse. The city was so named because of the shape of the hill (the Greeks changed the name to their own word). Under the Seleucids the city was called Antiochia. Emperor Augustus gave Hippos, along with Gadara, to Herod the Great. During excavations in 1948, four church buildings were uncovered. The long, column-lined, typical Roman main street, called a *cardo,* is discernible.

Gadara calls to mind the miracle of the demoniac. Matthew 8:28 mentions "Gergesenes" (KJV), while the New American Standard Bible has "Gadarenes"; Mark 5:1 and Luke 8:26 mention "Gadarenes" (KJV) while the New American Standard Bible has "Gerasenes." Thus, the ancient manuscripts have three words: Gergesenes, Gerasenes, and Gadarenes. Gergesa most likely is modern el-Kursi, on the upper east bank of the Sea of Galilee, and the most probable site for the miracle. Gerasa (Gerasenes) is a Decapolis city we will discuss shortly, much too far away to qualify for the miracle. Gadara is modern Umm Qeis, five or six miles southeast of the sea. A ship is portrayed on some of its coins, which likely indicates a connection with the sea. If so, the "country of the Gadarenes" could have run to the shoreline. The same argument of association could apply, of course, to Gerasa, but is less likely.

Gadara was an exceptionally strong fortress and an important city in the region. It had a university and its culture produced the poet Meleager, along with other famous writers. The ancient city is in ruins today, but still to be seen are two small theaters and some rock-cut tombs. The site boasts magnificent views north to the Sea of Galilee and south along the Jordan valley. The famous hot springs of Hammath, with their ruins of Roman and Byzantine baths, lie at the bottom of the Yarmuk gorge, just north of the city.

The city appears in history in 218 BC when it was captured by the Seleucid king Antiochus III. Alexander Jannaeus took it after a ten-month seige. Then Pompey "liberated" it in 63 BC, for the Romans. Shortly afterward Augustus gave it to Herod.

The massive Temple of Artemis (about AD 150) is the most imposing structure at Gerasa.

Abila lies east of Gadara; it also was a fortress and shared the fate of its neighbors. Antiochus III took it twice; during the Seleucid period it was called Seleucia. Abila's fate, however, was quite different. Today, as Irbid, it is Jordan's second largest city. The ancient site dates from about 2500 BC. Earlier in this century remnants of the thick, black basalt walls could be seen, but modern expansion has virtually eliminated the ruins. The Roman and Byzantine remains also have disappeared.

The next city, moving south, is in the foothills on the east side of the Jordan valley. Pella is of distinctive importance to Christians because the Jerusalem Christians moved there en masse just prior to the fall of Jerusalem. We would like very much to know why Pella was chosen by them. Excavations are currently in progress at *Tabaqat Fahl* (Pehal), across the Jordan and a bit south of Beth-shean. Findings so far have pushed habitation of the site back to about 5000 BC. Considerable work has been done on a Byzantine church building.

The early name Fahil dates back at least to the fifteenth century BC. The Seleucids changed the name to Pella, which was the name of Alexander the Great's birthplace in Macedonia. Macedonians probably were settled there at the time to establish the town as a Greek colony. Later, Ptolemy III Euergetes took the area for his Egyptian empire and changed the name to Berenice. Antiochus III recaptured the city for Seleucia in 218 BC and changed the name back to Pella. Alexander Jannaeus attacked Pella in 82 BC and demanded that the inhabitants convert to Judaism. When they refused, he destroyed the city. Pompey later rehabilitated it. Recent excavations have found evidence of Alexander Jannaeus' destruction of Pella and an uncovered street dates to Hellenistic times (about 332 BC to 160 BC in Palestine, though Greek influence continued).

ILLUSTRATOR PHOTO/KEN TOUCHTON

The Jerusalem Christians moved to Pella because of the deteriorating relationship between them and Jews after the martyrdom of James, the brother of Jesus. The flight may have included most Jerusalem Christians at one time or may have taken place over several years. Eusebius, an early church historian, tells us that prophets warned them to flee. Perhaps the majority went to Pella; perhaps they scattered more widely. At any rate, a Christian apologist named Ariston came out of Pella in the second century. During Byzantine times (about fourth to seventh centuries AD) Pella had its own bishop.

Gerasa (Jerash) lies in the mountains of Gilead, high above the Jordan River, south of Pella, and thirty miles from the Sea of Galilee. Its Roman ruins are the most fully preserved of any in the Middle East. The often-pictured marketplace (agora), the long, column-lined street, the temples, fountains, theater, and churches bespeak a glorious past (see photo 15, p. 72).

A stream called Chrysorhoas, which flows into the Jabbok, divides the city. Ancient habitation can be assumed wherever water is found. The area was home to ancient man as far back as 6000 BC. The town did not come into its own, though, until the Greeks conquered the East. Perdiccas, one of Alexander the Great's generals, may have established the city (in the Greek sense of organization). Antiochus IV Epiphanes (175-163 BC), who desecrated the Jerusalem Temple, may have refounded the city (conquerers liked to do that); it was called Antioch on the Chrysorhoas for a time. Alexander Jannaeus took it about 78 BC; then it came under Roman rule.

Rome opened up Gerasa to its greatest glory. Her architects redesigned the city to the point that no Hellenistic remains exist and the traces found indicate a complete change of layout. Gerasa was impressive in Jesus' day but reached its peak in the third century AD. Then a gradual decline started which lasted until the Persian invasion in 614 when the city was destroyed.

Christianity became dominant there, perhaps by the middle of the fourth century. Several church buildings were built then and later, especially during Justinian's reign. Its bishops participated in major decisions confronting Christianity. Recently, during reconstruction of the temple of Artemis, the earliest known Christian church building in Jordan was discovered. It dates to the first—second centuries.

ILLUSTRATOR PHOTO/KEN TOUCHTON

The last Decapolis city is situated south of Gerasa, at the southeastern edge of the Gilead mountains. It is Philadelphia, modern Amman, ancient Rabbath-Ammon, the Ammonite capital.

Amman is a very ancient, continuously-inhabited city which is mentioned often in the Old Testament. It became Greek under Ptolemy II (Philadelphus). The city was linked somehow with Tyre; perhaps Hellenized Tyrians were re-settled there. It is one of the strongest fortresses in Transjordan.

The Romans built Philadelphia along their own lines and in the process removed most evidence of earlier civilizations. The well-watered site was occupied during the Stone Age. The Hyksos controlled it about 1600 BC. It came under the Ammonites sometime after that and remained their capital throughout Old Testament times. Antiochus III captured the city for the Seleucids. When the Greek descendants grew weak, the Nabateans held the city for a time before they lost it to Herod about 30 BC.

Any continuously inhabited city is difficult to excavate, and remains tend to disappear over the centuries, the materials used in other buildings. Amman is such a city. Excavations, however, have been done on the citadel—the fortress which was within the ancient city. A theater that could seat 6,000 has been cleared, along with a smaller theater and a nymphaeum (large public fountain).

Left: The forum, 1*st* century AD was the market area of Gerasa. *Far left, bottom:* St. Theodore Cathedral, 4*th* century, was built over a temple of Dionysius. *Left, bottom:* Three adjoining church buildings, 7*th* century, commemorate SS. George, John, Cosmas, and Damian.

The Decapolis, then, consisted of cities scattered throughout present-day Jordan and the southern portion of the Golan Heights. The region was rich farmland, with some important trade routes passing through. The Greeks had spent over three hundred years by Jesus' day developing the culture of the region along Hellenistic lines.

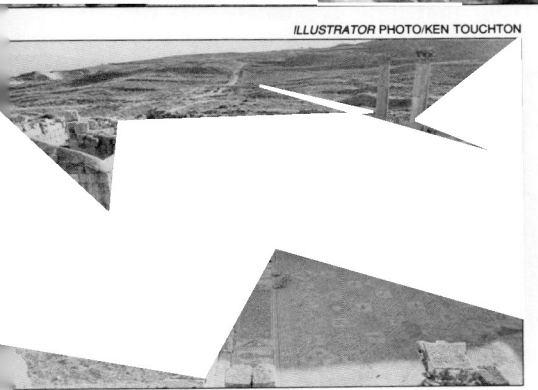

Perea, the last-mentioned region of Jesus' travels east of the Jordan, overlaps the Decapolis in territory. It was a narrow strip of land that ran along the Jordan River and to the east up the steep slopes and cliffs of the eastern mountains to include part of the fertile valleys of the Gilead hills. The north boundary was the Wadi Yabis just south of Pella; the south boundary was a chasm just north of the Arnon River that flows into the Dead Sea. The region included land along the Jordan that was at least as rich as California's Imperial Valley. It also included Amathus, Gerasa, Beth-aramphtha, Abila, Esbus, Machaerus (where John the Baptist was beheaded), and the hot springs of Callirrhoe (where Herod the Great went often for relief in the time just before his death).

Amathus was a strong fortress on a wadi just north of the Jabbok River and on a line with Gerasa. Beth-aramphtha was ancient Beth-haram. Fortified by Herod, it was burned a few years later to quell a revolt. Herod Antipas rebuilt it, called it Livias (changing it to Julias when Caesar's wife changed her name), and made it his center of power in the region. Today it is Tell er-Rameh. Abila is Old Testament Abel-shittim (Tell Kefrein) just north of the Dead Sea. Esbus was the descendant city of Old Testament Heshbon. Machaerus was Herod Antipas' southernmost fortress, designed to protect against the Nabateans. The hot springs of Callirrhoe are on the eastern shore of the Dead Sea, not far from Machaerus.

Perea is not mentioned often in ancient records, but we know that many Jews lived there in Jesus' day. Bible students have heard of it most often as the territory to which Jews crossed over to avoid going through Samaria. It includes parts of the areas given to the tribes of Gad and Reuben. Its fortunes rose and fell through Old Testament history, depending on the relative strength of Israel, Syria, and the Ammonites (see photo 14, p. 72).

During the Persian occupation, a family called the Tobiads rose to a position of power. They were from the area later called Perea, from a home near Ammon. Nehemiah forced a Tobiad out of his quarters in the Temple; the Tobiads teamed with Sanballat, governor of Samaria, to keep Nehemiah from building the walls of Jerusalem. Over the years the Tobiad family gained prestige among the Judeans and were quite influential in the power plays between the Ptolemies of Egypt and the Seleucids of Syria for control over Palestine. Their ancestral fortress-palace just west of Amman is impressive even in ruin. The site is Araq el-Emir in the beautiful valley called Wadi Syr. During these centuries the links between Judea and Perea apparently were strengthened.

Herod the Great was granted Perea by Mark Antony about 39 BC. Herod's brother Pheroras administered the region; then later his cousin Ahiab.

After Herod died, one of his slaves, Simon, attempted a rebellion and named himself king of Perea. The Roman general Varus responded by quickly breaking the revolt and crucifying two thousand Jews of Transjordan. This is the event in which Beth-aramptha (Julias) was burned.

Herod Antipas, who received the region along with Galilee, ruled in relative peace. After his death, Perea was included in the province of Judea. From that time on, the region was involved in the growing unrest that led finally to the Jewish revolt of AD 66-70.

Perea was a rich region then as now, primarily trading in sheep and wool. The agricultural output, too, was impressive, particularly in the semitropical Jordan valley.

These, then, are the lands in which Jesus traveled and worked beyond Judea and Galilee. The climate then was about as now, but the land was richer, a vision which the Jordan government has seen and toward which it works.

Jerusalem

Above: Roman steps leading to Caiaphas' House.
Right: Church structure being built over excavated Caiaphas' House.

William H. Stephens

Major General Sir Charles Warren, crawling on his stomach, held a candle in his mouth for light. He pulled himself along a few inches at a time through the wet tunnel. At any time a flow of water could trap and drown him, along with his companion, Sergeant Birtles, who followed behind. Some 1,700 feet later, they emerged unhurt at the Pool of Siloam. They had discovered Hezekiah's tunnel.

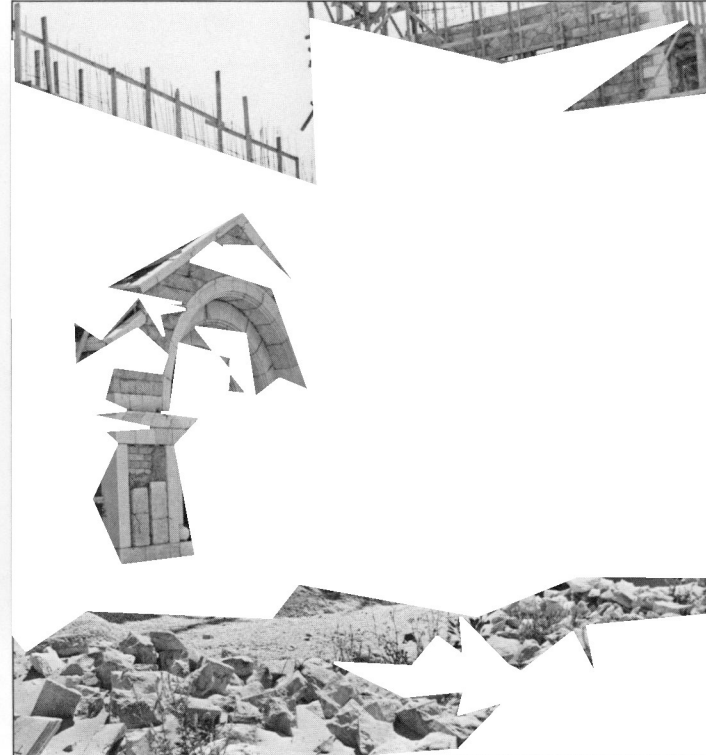

The year was 1867, the dawn of archeology in Jerusalem. A generation had passed since Edward Robinson, an American, had conducted a scientific survey of Palestine. The methods of Warren and others sent from England by the new Palestine Exploration Fund were primitive and daring, including dangerous tunneling around the walls of the Old City. But they began the process of excavating what is probably the most difficult site anywhere.

We have learned much about Jerusalem since then; and though many intriguing questions remain for future years, the history of Jerusalem is gradually being pieced together.

The earliest written record we have for Jerusalem is from the Egyptian Execration Texts (names of enemies were written on clay, cursed, then smashed to magically aid the curse). They date from the period 1800-1600 BC and read *Rushalimum*. In the Tell el-Amarna tablets, from the 1300s BC, the name is *Urusalim*. The city probably was named for Shalem, the god of the setting sun.[1]

While that earliest reference dates back to about the eighteenth century BC, archeologists have uncovered sherds (pottery pieces) that date to about 3000 BC, the early Bronze Age. Tombs that date from the same period also have been excavated. Jerusalem, whatever its name then, was only of moderate importance. The people were living in caves and mud huts on the slope of Ophel (the southeastern hill), where they had access to the water of the Gihon Spring, with a small settlement on the hill's summit.[2]

Kathleen Kenyon believes the early-Bronze-Age Jerusalem was destroyed, perhaps by nomads who continued to stop there for several centuries. Her famous excavations, along with the Execration Texts, indicate that Jerusalem probably was a walled city by 1800 BC. The people who occupied Jerusalem of that period included Melchizedek, to whom Abraham paid a tithe. They met in the area of en-Rogel, a spring well where the Kidron and Hinnom valleys join (Gen. 14:17). Evidence from tombs tells us that the city had a trade relationship with Cyprus and Mycenae.[3] By the time of the el-Amarna Letters, Jerusalem was a leading city of Canaan, loyal to a weakened Egypt, and having considerable difficulty both with marauders and with Egyptian soldiers who apparently were not being paid adequately.

By the time Joshua began the Conquest, Jerusalem was inhabited by Jebusites and was called Jebus. The Bible gives hints that these people were either Hittites or people from the north who were displaced during an upheaval of populations about that time. The history of this period is still confused. At any rate, they apparently built terraces on the east slope of Ophel to enlarge its size, and they built a strong wall.

One of the Jebusite kings, Adoni-zedek, led several Amorite kings against Joshua to try to retrieve Gibeon, a strong ally to Jebus before she surrendered to the Hebrews (Josh. 9). Joshua won the battle but did not conquer Jerusalem (Josh. 10). After Joshua died, the tribes of Judah and Simeon attacked Jebus' army, captured King Adoni-bezek, mutilated him to the point that he could no longer be a warrior, and allowed him to return to Jerusalem (Judg. 1:1-8). Either then or later they attacked Jerusalem and set it afire, but they must not have destroyed the walled city itself, for we find it still independent later.

The walled Jerusalem, during those early centuries before David, occupied some ten acres on the spur called Ophel that runs south of the present southeast corner of the Temple Mount. The Tyropean Valley is shallow today but then was about as steep as the Kidron Valley. The two valleys—the Kidron on the east and the Tyropean on the west—joined at the south end of Ophel, making the hill wedge-shaped. The city was well situated for trade, which moved

ILLUSTRATOR PHOTO/KEN TOUCHTON

The Hinnom Valley, Jerusalem's city dump south of the city, became the figure for hell (Ge-henna).

Left: The lower courses were a part of Herod's palace, possibly the tower of Phasael. *Bottom:* A square tower, built by the Maccabees John Hyrcanus or Alexander Jannaeus, 130-100 BC.

from the Jordan Valley to the east and joined various roads that funnel out to the west. Other roads came from the south from points beyond Hebron to move north to Damascus and cities like Tyre.

The Gihon Spring continued to be the city's chief water source, which explains why the settlers built on Ophel rather than one of the higher hills on three sides. By the time of the judges, the inhabitants had cut a shaft and tunnel from the city walls to connect with the Gihon. It was up this shaft that Joab climbed to surprise the Jebusites (see photo 18, p. 105) and take the city in about 1000 BC.

That story is told succinctly in 2 Samuel 5:6-10, more clearly in the Revised Standard Version. With a little imagination by the reader to fill out the drama, the genius of this military operation becomes very impressive.

Jerusalem was a perfect choice as David's capital city for three reasons: (1) By conquest, it was his personal royal city. (2) It was well located between the southern tribes he had ruled for seven years and the northern tribes that were just beginning to acknowledge him king. (3) Jerusalem was neutral territory since it belonged to no tribe, somewhat like our Washington, D.C.

Kenyon's excavations indicate that the Jebusite walls continued to be used at least until the eighth century BC.[4] David apparently strengthened and extended the Millo, which must have been the terraces found by Kenyon on the east slope of Ophel. The location shown on some Bible maps that indicates an area between Ophel and the Temple Mount is incorrect. Though he did not build the Temple, David embarked on an elaborate building program for his new capital (2 Sam. 5:11; 1 Chron. 11:7-8). When he purchased the threshing floor of Araunah the Jebusite—who probably was a prince allowed to live after the capture of Jerusalem[5]—and moved the ark of the covenant there, he took the first giant step in making Jerusalem the worship center of Israel.

Solomon pursued David's dream, which the Bible tells us was the will of God. He built the Temple first, then the palace complex to the south, joining the Temple on one side and the City of David on the other. The palace complex was massive, containing his personal quarters, the house of Pharaoh's daughter (his queen), the house of the cedars of Lebanon (which Mazar believes may have been an arsenal), and the house of the throne (main ceremonial hall). The area may also have housed his many wives and concubines. He also repaired the Millo, which must have required constant upkeep.

Jerusalem expanded under the kings who succeeded Solomon, even though Judah usually was the poorer of the two divided kingdoms. Its population likely was swelled after the fall of the Northern Kingdom in 722 BC. Unfortunately, the expanded environs included shrines to pagan gods as well as to Yahweh. Kenyon found a cache of objects and vessels used in pagan worship, which she believes was stored there about 700 BC,[6] which would be toward the end of Hezekiah's reign. Others propose the cache to date to Josiah's reform about 620 BC, supposing that he caused the objects to be dumped there.[7]

By the time Jerusalem was threatened by Babylon, suburbs had spread to the west across the Tyropean to the western hill. The valley suburb was called the Makhtesh (hollow); the western hill was called the Mishneh (Second Quarter; see 2 Kings 22:14). The walls probably were extended to include these areas during the eighth and seventh centuries. About half of the expansions were inside the present Old City, about half south of the present city wall.

Hezekiah's building achievements were tied heavily to defense but the city grew due to economics too. He strengthened the walls and apparently added a stretch to include the Pool of Siloam (this point is debated but seems probable). He was the one who had the tunnel dug described at the beginning of this article (See "The Gihon and the Pool of Siloam," p. 122).

Other kings, such as Manasseh, continued the policy of strengthening the city walls. The work was well done, for Jerusalem stood the seige of Babylon from the spring of 587 until the invaders broke through the northern wall in August of 586. The story of three successive deportations to Babylon and the total destruction of the city and Temple reflects a crucial period in the history of Israel (see photo 24, p. 108).

About seventy years later, the various peoples conquered by Babylon were allowed to return to their homelands by the new master of the East, Cyrus of Persia (see photo 13, p. 72). The first group of Jews returned under the leadership of Sheshbazzar, but they quickly became dispirited after doing only some foundation work on the Temple. Another generation went by before Zerubbabel led a large group back to their Promised Land. A grandson of Jehoiachin, he was held by some to be the messiah. Appointed governor of Judah and aided by a high priest named Joshua, he led the people to rebuild the Temple. It was begun in 520 BC and completed

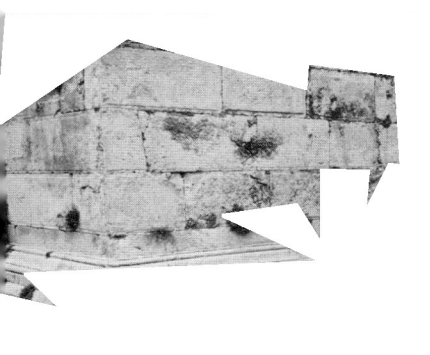

ILLUSTRATOR PHOTO/DAVID ROGERS
This smaller gate and wall, located beside and below the Damascus Gate, almost surely was part of the third wall built by Herod Agrippa I about AD 41-42.

on March 3, 515 (Ezra 6:15). We may assume that it was but a shadow of Solomon's magnificent structure, but it was the longest-lasting of the three Temples, serving Jerusalem from 515 until Herod built his near the time of Christ.

The resettlers of Jerusalem were hard put to rebuild their lives and their city. Much of the story is told in Ezra and Nehemiah. Otherwise, evidence is slim for the Persian period, which lasted until 332 BC and the arrival of Alexander the Great. Apparently Jerusalem was a small semiautonomous temple state under the rule of the Fifth Satrap of Persia. Nothing remains today of Solomon's Temple or of Zerubbabel's (which must have been elaborated during its five centuries of existence), but a joint in the eastern wall reveals the line where Herod enlarged the mount.

With the arrival of the Greeks, both Jerusalem and its culture faced great challenges. The city switched hands several times between rule by the Ptolemies and the Seleucids. The office of high priest assumed the function of governor and thus entered full-fledged into power politics. The aggressive efforts of the Greek rulers to introduce their culture into all the lands they conquered created sharp divisions among the Jews. Jerusalem, for a time, was called Antioch-in-Jerusalem after Antiochus, the Seleucid (Greek) King. Sometime during this general period, a gymnasium was built in the area of the present-day plaza by the Western (Wailing) Wall. Apparently the gymnasium was destroyed by the Maccabees (see below) and a flat courtyard area called the Xystos built over it. The so-called Masonic Hall was part of this de-

This wide-angle view of area south of the Temple Mount shows extent of current excavations, which reveal Moslem, Christian, and Jewish structures.

stroyed gymnasium.[8] Finally, when Antiochus IV Epiphanes forced the issue and sacrificed a swine on the altar in Jerusalem, raised a statue to Zeus in the Temple, and tried to suppress Jewish worship, a revolution started. First Maccabees, a book included in the Apocrypha, tells the story of the revolt and its progress. The Maccabee family—the Hasmoneans—led a successful revolt against the crumbling Seleucids and carved out a more or less independent nation. Finally, in 164 BC, the Maccabees gained by negotiation the hated Seleucid fortress called the Akra. They destroyed it; now we do not even know where it stood.

Jerusalem prospered greatly under the Maccabees. They built walls and otherwise fortified the city, and the city expanded (see photo 21, p. 106). The prosperity of the period can be seen in the architecture of the tombs in the Kidron Valley. The Beni Hazir mausoleum is a tomb complex built by a wealthy family of the Maccabean period (see photo 28, p. 110).

The Hasmoneans, however, rather quickly fell into the kingship pattern of the day, ruling almost despotically, forcing Gentiles in surrounding territories to convert to Judaism or be killed. Alexander Jannaeus, under whom Jerusalem and Judah grew significantly, was especially aggressive in this regard.

The last years of the Maccabean rule were confusing and tragic ones. Queen Salome Alexandra, who ruled ably, was the last ruler before disintegration took over completely. Even before she died, the potential heirs began their disastrous maneuvering which degenerated into warfare between two brothers, Hyrcanus and Aristobulus. Hyrcanus had an influential friend who advised him shrewdly, reading the changing Roman scene well enough to place Hyrcanus and himself in a favorable position. The adviser was Antipater, the father of Herod.

Pompey, the Roman general who solved the piracy problem in the eastern Mediterranean and subjugated the Eastern countries, captured the fortress called the Birah at the northwest corner of the Temple Mount in 63 BC. Further battles continued, but Rome took the city completely in 57 BC. Antipater became the power behind Hyrcanus, who was confirmed by Rome as high priest, thus the nominal ruler of Judea. Antipater continued his shrewd reading of international politics over the years that followed; the result was that Herod eventually was named king by Caesar.

Herod had to fight for his throne however. Backed by Roman swords, Herod broke through Jerusalem's north walls and captured the Temple and the Upper City—ironically, on the Day of Atonement, 37 BC.

Herod was an energetic builder. He also found ways to amass enormous personal wealth. Strapped for funds when he began his conquest of his new kingdom, in a short time he had found ways to milk enough funds from his subjects and holdings to begin his building projects. He spent money for projects in many places outside Palestine. Jerusalem, though, was considerably transformed by his efforts. (See "Herod's Temple," p. 142, for a discussion of the Temple Mount.) In addition to the Temple, he built his (1) royal palace, which extended from the Citadel area of present day Jerusalem to the southwest corner of the Old City, including the massive towers of Hippicus, Phasael, and Mariamne (the foundation of Phasael has been identified near the so-called Tower of David); (2) the fortress Antonia (rebuilt; see "Judgment Hall," p. 163); (3) a series of tombs, located near the present day King David Hotel; (4) a memorial over the entrance to David's tomb; (5) five porticoes of the Pool of Bethesda (see "The Pool of Bethesda," p. 118); (6) a theater, probably on the east slope of the Upper City; (7) a stadium or hippodrome south of the Temple Mount.

According to one authority, "At his death Herod left behind him a demoralized populace with weakened morality, resigned to misfortune."[9] When he died, a delegation went to Rome to demand removal of the Greeks from their places of influence. These "Greeks" were probably Hellenized members of Herod's retinue. Herod's son and successor, Archelaus, was worse than his father. Caesar Augustus deposed him in AD 6 and made Judea a province.

In spite of the intrigues and inequities in Jerusalem, the city continued to develop after Herod's death. Public life in Jerusalem in Jesus' day was dominated by the court of the Herodian family. Herod had organized sports game to take place in Jerusalem every four years. The royal family determined the trends, and their habits brought an influx of luxury goods into the city.

The city's population during the first century has been widely estimated from 25,000 to 125,000. Most scholars lean toward the latter figure, which would include the suburbs and outlying villages. The city area occupied something like 450 acres.[10] Olive oil was the chief export—olive trees were larger and more extensive in Jesus' day than now—but other industries included most of the products and services one would expect in the pilgrim city.

This massive stairway along the south wall of the Temple was the one Jesus climbed to enter the Double or Triple Gates.

ILLUSTRATOR PHOTO/DAVID ROGERS

Quarrying of stone was a major industry at Jerusalem, stimulated by the extensive building projects and the demand for tombs (Jews from all over the world sought burial in the Holy City). The tombs of the Herodian period, in fact, tell us something of the Jerusalem of Jesus' day. The well-known tombs in the Kidron Valley already have been mentioned. The Tomb of Absalom and Tomb of Jehoshaphat date to the beginning of the first century AD and reflect the cosmopolitanism of the wealthy class. Jason's Tomb to the west of the Old City dates to the first century BC; it belonged to a seafaring family, not a usual occupation for Jews in their prior history. The tombs of the family of Nicanor of Alexandria, Egypt, who donated the doors for the Nicanor Gate, have been found on Mount Scopus. Another tomb, of Simon the Temple Builder, contained the bones of a man who had been crucified, providing new information on this heinous method of execution. Many more tombs have been found, for cemeteries literally ringed the city.

Jerusalem was not well situated to be as large as it was. Consequently, water was a problem and ingenious solutions were found. The Gihon was inadequate but continued its supply. In addition, vast cisterns have been discovered, especially under and around the Temple Mount, particularly the Struthion Cistern near the Fortress Antonia, the Pool of the Towers ("Hezekiah's Pool") north of the Citadel area, the Israel Pool just north of the Temple Mount, and vast underground reservoirs for the Temple. Pilate created a serious incident when he confiscated the Temple treasury to build an aqueduct from "Solomon's Pools" in the south to Jerusalem, but the city benefited greatly so far as water was concerned.

During Jesus' day the walls of Jerusalem followed a different line than they do now. The Ophel hill south of the Temple Mount was included within the walls, which ran below the Pool of Siloam, then turned west to include the present Zion, which today lies outside the walls.

The first-century wall then turned north to join, on a parallel line, the present southwest corner. The northern walls are uncertain. It probably ran east from the Citadel (Herod's Palace; see photo 17, p. 105), then turned north to encircle an area between the Citadel and the Temple Mount, then joined the fortress Antonia. The site of the present Church of the Holy Sepulcher almost certainly was outside the walls. Later, King Agrippa I started another wall to enclose the large area of Bezetha north and northwest of the Temple Mount. A small but tasteful gate to this wall has been uncovered under the present Damascus Gate. The Romans made him stop construction, perhaps fearing his motive. Later still, during the Jewish revolt of AD 66-70, the Jews hurriedly completed the wall.

ILLUSTRATOR PHOTO/DAVID ROGERS

The Upper City, the Lower City, Ophel, and the Temple thus were included within the walls in Jesus' day. The valleys of Hinnom and Kidron bounded the walls on the southwest, south, and east. The Typropean ran between the Upper City and the Lower. Only one bridge crossed it, connecting with the ancient arch on the western wall called Wilson's Arch.

ILLUSTRATOR PHOTO/DAVID ROGERS

The structures on the massive Temple Mount were destroyed in AD 70. Even the paving-stones date to Moslem times, but the size of the mount is as Herod built it.

The Upper City was the more prosperous section; excavations have uncovered first-century houses that indicate that the area was closely built-up.[11] An upper-class house has been found, and another house belonging to the important priestly Kathros family; the latter was burned in the AD 70 destruction. Other Herodian period houses also have been found. The palace of the Hasmoneans, rebuilt by Agrippa I, and the palace of the high priest Ananias were in the Upper City.

The Essenes may have had a section in first-century Jerusalem, along with a certain gate they used which allowed them to follow strict rules of purity. The tradespeople and the poorer people lived and worked in the Lower City. Agrippa I (AD 37-44) probably was responsible for establishing two major market areas, one in the upper part and one in the lower part of the Tyropean Valley. Agrippa II (AD 48-70), whose reign was delayed for a while after his father died because Caesar thought he was too young, completed the Temple, leaving 18,000 workers unemployed. He put them to work paving the streets with white stone. Some of these pavements have been uncovered.

The streets of Jerusalem were carefully cared for. Indeed, the cleanliness of the entire city was important since Jerusalem was a religious center in which rules of purity were so strict. The roads were swept every day.[12] Drainage canals were built of such efficiency that they have continued working even up to modern times, in spite of the fact that they were lost to history for centuries. The industries that produced heavy refuse were located near the Hinnom Valley (the city dump), and the Dung Gate opened to the Hinnom (see photo 22, p. 105).

A synagogue was discovered several decades ago by the early excavator, Weill, on the Ophel hill. Here was found the famous Theodotian Stone, telling who built the synagogue. Some have thought it was the "synagogue of the Libertines" (Acts 6:9) whose members stoned Stephen and to which Paul (Saul) belonged,[13] while others believe it was not built until AD 65.[14] Of course, the two views are not mutually exclusive.

Jerusalem was destroyed in AD 70. The events that led to that catastrophe were complex. Titus, the Roman general, faced Jerusalem with four full legions (about 6,000 soldiers each, plus cavalry). He established his headquarters on Mount Scopus and attacked from the north. He had to break through the wall Agrippa had built; then he had another wall to face, the older one linked to the Antonia; then he had the Temple itself, a massive fortress in its own right. At that point, he had his troops construct a wall all the way around the city, established thirteen fortified camps from which to patrol the wall continuously, and then he waited for the feuding factions in the Temple to defeat themselves.

The siege brought about terrible famine combined with a cruel and disastrous civil war. Finally, after many months, Titus took the city with unmerciful slaughter, attested to by bones and skulls that have been found.[15] Excavations have verified the thoroughness of the fall of Jerusalem. The once-deep Tyropean Valley was made shallow by the masonry blocks and debris dumped into it. Pavements built by the Ommayad Moslems (AD 660-750) at the south end of the western wall are built on top of rubble and silt thirteen feet deep that covered the Herodian street.

Titus left the Tenth Legion to watch over the conquered Judea. Jews continued to live as best they could in the destroyed city, and synagogue services were allowed to continue. However, the unrest continued to simmer until, sixty-two years later, it broke out again in the revolt led by Simon Bar-Kochba. This time the city not only was destroyed but its surrounding lands were plowed up.

Hadrian was the Roman emperor of the time. He determined to put an end to Jewish Jerusalem. To do so, he forbade Jews to live in the city and rebuilt Jerusalem as a Roman colony, changing its name to Aelia Capitolina (Aelia was his middle name). He built several

(continued on p. 113)

Top: The sixth-century Madeba mosaic map shows Jerusalem as Hadrian had it rebuilt (note columned street). *Left:* Excavations near David's Tower have revealed several periods of occupation. *Above:* The sloping masonry has now been identified as a Jebusite ramp. The square structure at far right of photo was part of Nehemiah's wall.

Right: Juncture of Hinnom and Kidron Valleys, with Mount of Olives beyond. *Below:* Lush Jericho region with hills of Perea beyond.

Opposite: The Dome of the Rock covers the stone on which the altar or Temple stood. *Above:* Jerusalem seen from Mount of Olives. *Left:* Defensive tower built by Maccabees in Jerusalem's city wall.

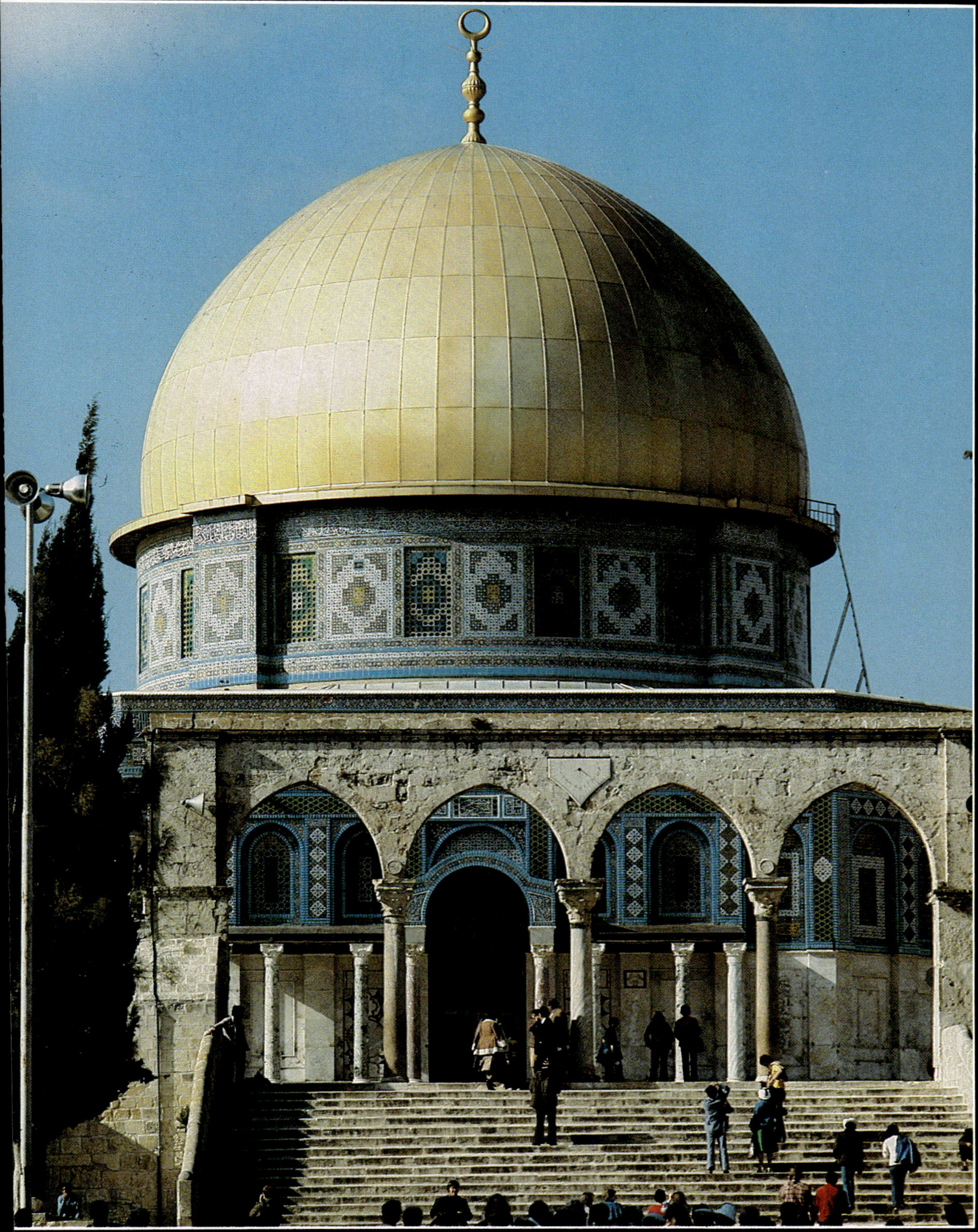

ILLUSTRATOR PHOTO/DAVID ROGERS

Top: 7th-century steps on east slope of Ophel, destroyed by Babylonians. *Above:* Jordan Valley and region of Decapolis beyond, shot from Beth-shean. *Right:* Traditional Upper Room; construction is 14th century but location is probable.

ILLUSTRATOR PHOTO:KEN TOUCHTON

ILLUSTRATOR PHOTO/DAVID ROGERS

ILLUSTRATOR PHOTO/KEN TOUCHTON

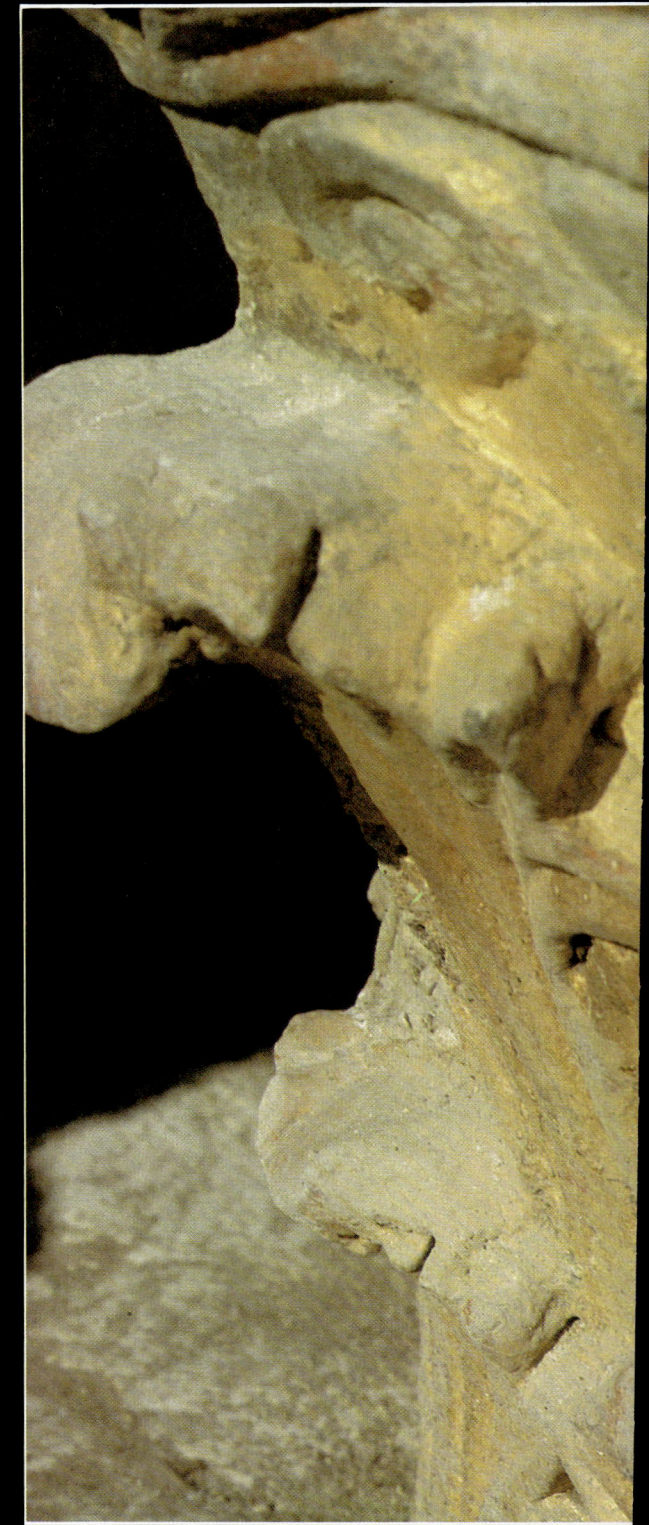

110

Opposite, top: Queen Eudocia's palace was located in area shown. *Opposite, bottom:* The Beni Hezir tomb reveals the prosperity of Jerusalem during Maccabean and Herodian rule. *Center:* Capital from Herod's Temple with gold leaf still intact. *Above:* Traditional Golden Gate (Shushan Gate) whose exact location is disputed.

111

Left: Churches on Gethsemane slope: Dominus Flevit (dominant): Russian Church of St. Mary Magdalene (onion domes). *Above:* The empty interior of the Garden Tomb symbolizes Jesus' resurrection.

A closed-up portion of the massive Double Gate of Jesus' day.

A ritual bath (*mikvah*) between Double and Triple Gates for ritual cleansing.

pagan shrines and temples, including one of the Temple Mount, each placed so as to desecrate a sacred site. He rebuilt the city along Roman lines; some present-day streets follow the lines his engineers established (see photo 16, p. 105). A portion of the long north to south street called the Cardo has been uncovered.

As the Byzantine period began in the fourth century with the emporer Constantine, Jerusalem fast became a major Christian center of pilgrimage. Only briefly, during the rule of Julian the Apostate (AD 362-363) were Jews back in control of the city. Christian emperors expended great sums of money to construct elaborate buildings over Christian holy places.

The Persians conquered the land in the seventh century, destroying the Christian churches and erecting mosques in their turn. The Crusaders returned the favor in the twelfth century and for almost a hundred years held sway in Palestine. In 1187 the Arab conqueror Saladin retook Jerusalem. It remained Moslem until the British Mandate.

The many revered sites in and around Jerusalem reflect the vicissitudes of the city. Some sites are accurately identified, some are not. One of the ways accuracy is determined is through excavating to discover when a shrine first was built over a site. The earlier a shrine was built, the more probable is the tradition to be true.

113

ILLUSTRATOR PHOTO/DAVID ROGERS

The so-called Tombs of the Kings actually comprise the Tomb of Queen Helena of Adiabene (a district on the upper Tigris river). *Large photo:* Monumental stairway. *Right:* Entrance.

The most important sites in Jerusalem for Christians are the places of Jesus' crucifixion and burial (See "Where Is Golgotha?" p. 168). The Church of the Holy Sepulcher almost certainly covers both of the sites. When Hadrian desecrated the Jewish holy places, he treated the Christian ones with the same disrespect. Eusebius tells us that Hadrian covered over Jesus' burial place with earth, paved over that, and then erected a shrine to Venus. He would not have done so if the site was not revered.[16]

The emperor Constantine (330-337) ordered the earth removed and a Christian church built. The natural stone of the hill of Calvary and of Christ's tomb were cut away to leave only the small areas where the cross and the tomb chamber were. The Church of the Holy

ILLUSTRATOR PHOTO/DAVID ROGERS

Sepulcher, which has been added to and altered over the centuries, is exceptionally large and covers both sites.

Several other churches were built during the fourth century to commemorate holy sites: the Eleona in AD 326 and perhaps the Church of the Ascension in the same century (See "Where Did the Ascension Take Place?" p. 182), the

Left: Rooftops of Church of the Holy Sepulchre. Largest dome is over tomb; smaller dome almost above Chapel of St. Helena; square bell tower in right foreground. *Bottom:* Cloister converted from Eudocia's palace (see photo 42, p. 111) with well-formed doorways and arches.

Church of the Agony in AD 385 (See "Gethsemane and the Mount of Olives," p. 157), and the Hagia Zion, the "Mother of All Churches," in AD 340. This last one was the early structure of the *Coenaculum,* the traditional site of the Lord's Supper on Mount Zion.

Recent excavations along the south wall of the Temple Mount have uncovered a cloister that could house 600 nuns (see photo 42, p. 111); earlier it may have been the palace of Queen Eudocia, the estranged wife of the emperor Theodosius II (401-450). Eudocia spent large sums of money on Christian structures in Jerusalem, in addition to expanding the city walls. The basilica (a cathedral-type structure) found several decades ago by the Pool of Siloam was built by her, as was the church dedicated to Saint Stephen, located outside the present Damascus Gate, and a lodging for the aged on Mount Scopus.[17]

Jerusalem's next period of expansion came under Emperor Justinian (483-565), who enlarged many church buildings around Palestine. He built the massive Nea church in Jerusalem, a portion which has been excavated (see photo).

Many other sites of vital interest to Christians are commemorated in Jerusalem (see photo 43, p. 111). Indeed, an entire month of sight-seeing probably would not cover all of the important places. The most crucial, though, are within and near the Old City. Along the southern exposure of the wall, excavations can be seen from the road, including a wide staircase that leads up to the partially blocked Double Gate. Kenyon's excavations can be seen southeast of the Mount, as can the Gihon Spring, the Pool of Siloam, and en-Rogel. Mount Zion is southwest of the city wall, with the traditional Tomb of David, the Upper Room, Caiaphas' House, and Roman steps. At the southwest corner of the Temple Mount are mixed ruins of Herodian, Roman, and early Arab structures. On the west wall, the Jaffa Gate gives entrance to the Old City next to the Citadel area, where the traditional Tower of David marks more important and authentic ruins that date back to Maccabean times.

Bottom: A corner of a Byzantine church called the Nea has been excavated protruding from the Old City's south wall.

Many of the other sites have already been described. The Church of the Holy Sepulcher is west of the Temple Mount and roughly midway between the Jaffa and Damascus Gates. The Via Dolorosa, the Fortress Antonia, the Pool of Israel, and St. Anne's Church (Crusader period) next to the ancient Pool of Bethesda all are north of the Temple Mount but inside the city walls.

Artifacts from the excavations are displayed in Jerusalem's museums, especially the Rockefeller (Palestine) Archaeological Museum.

A tour to Jerusalem is a highlight for any Christian. To see the places where biblical events actually happened has a way of verifying them in the traveler's mind.

[1] B. Mazar, "Jerusalem in the Biblical Period," *Jerusalem Revealed*, (The Israel Exploration Society, Jerusalem, 1975), p. 1.
[2] Kathleen M. Kenyon, *Digging Up Jerusalem* (New York: Praeger Publishers, 1974), pp. 78-79.
[3] Benjamin Mazar, *The Mountain of the Lord* (Garden City, New York: Doubleday and Company, Inc., 1975), p. 47.
[4] Kenyon, p. 100.
[5] Mazar, p. 5
[6] Kenyon, pp. 133-143.
[7] Mazar, p. 58.
[8] Ibid. p. 220.
[9] Joachim Jeremias, *Jerusalem in the Time of Jesus* (Philadelphia: Fortress Press, 1969), p. 125.
[10] Mazar, p. 210.
[11] Kenyon, p. 237.
[12] Jeremias, p. 17.
[13] Ibid., pp. 65-66.
[14] Mazar, p. 87.
[15] Kenyon, pp. 250-254.
[16] Jack Finegan, *The Archeology of the New Testament* (Princeton, New Jersey: Princeton University Press, 1969), pp. 137-138, 164.
[17] Mazar, p. 254.

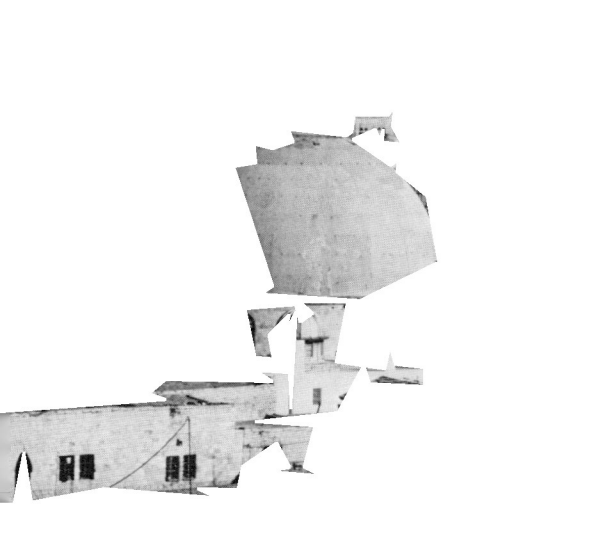

ILLUSTRATOR PHOTO/DAVID ROGERS

The Pool of Bethesda

FOREIGN MISSION BOARD, SBC/FON SCOFIELD

Elmer L. Gray

As Jesus walked through the arched doorway, he entered a porch along one side of a large, twin-pool complex. The doorway was in the middle of the wall enclosing the area. The porch which served as a passageway and as a lounging space stretched approximately 150 feet to each side of the doorway.

Immediately in front of Jesus extended a second covered porch that provided a walkway between the two pools to yet a third porch like the one he had entered. Also, each end of the pool complex boasted a porch, making a total of five porches around and dividing the pools.

The porches surrounding the pools consisted of a roof supported on the outer side by a wall and on the pool side by columns thirty feet high. The center porch dividing the pools had a roof supported on both sides by the graceful columns.

The pools were not equal in size. One side was perpendicular to the ends whereas the other was at an angle, making the complex a little over 150 feet wide at one end and over 200 feet wide at the other end.

This was the Pool of Bethesda, where Jesus healed the man who had been ill for thirty-eight years.

As archeology developed in the nineteenth century, researchers attempted to identify more and more biblical sites. The location of the Pool of Bethesda was not known. Some scholars had thought that the Bethesda Pool might have been the same as the Pool of Siloam, but a site unearthed in the latter part of the nineteenth century gives strong evidence of being the Pool of Bethesda.

In 1888 Conrad Schick, digging on the property of St. Anne's Church, unearthed twin pools and became convinced he had found the Pool of Bethesda. Further excavation in 1923 revealed more of the site. Then in the mid-1960s archeologists exposed enough of the area for the viewer to appreciate the beauty of the original pool.

In Jesus' day, this pool was located in a section of Jerusalem north of the city wall. That

ÉCOLE BIBLIQUE ET ARCHÉOLOGIQUE FRANCAISE

Above: The Crusader period Church of St. Anne (Mary's mother). *Opposite:* Excavations at St. Anne's; under the apse (curved wall) of the Crusader chapel ruins lie Byzantine ruins and a Roman cistern; under those ruins lie part of the twin pools of Bethesda.

section was known as Bezetha after the Brook of Bezetha, which had been a major source of water for the city before the time of Herod the Great.

During the reign of Herod Agrippa—the Herod before whom Paul appeared—the city wall was extended to incorporate the district of Bezetha.

The name of the Pool of Bethesda may have developed from the name of the district. In some of the oldest manuscripts the pool's name appears as Bethzatha and is so spelled in *Today's English Version*. Because of the miracle Jesus performed there the Christians may have referred to the pool as Bethesda, "House of Mercy," and this name could have been inserted by later copyists of the early manuscripts. In any case, some scholars explain the name Bethesda in this manner.

The pool was built, or at least enclosed, with the porches by Herod the Great. Therefore, by the time Jesus visited it in the years of his ministry the pool was at least over thirty years old.

Herod had filled in the Brook of Bezetha where it flowed by the mount on which he had rebuilt the Temple. He had done this with fill from his project of leveling and extending the top of the mount in order to expand the Temple area. He had, in fact, one of the most ambitious building programs of any ruler in history. His building projects included a number of reservoirs in Jerusalem to improve the city's water supply. Not only did he fill in the lower section of the Bezetha Brook to widen the mountain platform for the Temple but he also walled several sections of the brook for pools, the best known of which were the Sheep Pool and the Pool of Israel. The Pool of Israel was one of Jerusalem's largest reservoirs. Approximately thirty feet deep, it was located immediately adjacent to the northeast corner of the Temple area.

The Sheep Pool, perhaps so-called because it was on the route where animals were herded to the Temple for sacrifice, cannot be equated definitely with the Pool of Bethzatha and later the Pool of Bethesda. However, evidence from Greek manuscripts of John 5:2 and from Eusebius (*Onomasticon*, p. 58) make this conclusion plausible.

When Herod walled this pool in and built the beautiful porches, the pool was divided into twin basins, one for men and one for women. Pilgrims traveling to worship at the Temple probably used the pools for ritualistic bathing. The pool may have been the most popular public bath in Jerusalem.

The Bethesda Pool was about 250 yards north of a gate in the northern wall of the Temple courtyard. This Sheep Gate, according to Nehemiah 3:1, was built by priests probably to serve as a major entrance into the Temple area. Perhaps it was originally so named because sacrificial sheep were purchased at the nearby sheep market and driven through the gate into the Temple area. The gate was just east of the Tower of Antonia, the guard fortress where Roman soldiers were stationed to oversee the goings-on in the Temple courtyard.

Jesus' attention focused on a man who had been sick for thirty-eight years who lay on one of the five porches. Jesus asked the man if he wanted to be healed. The man really never answered Jesus' question. He did say that no one would help him get into the water when it was bubbling. The pool evidently continued to be fed by water moving underground in the area of the former Brook of Bezetha.

In New Testament times the pool had the reputation of being a place where supernatural healings occurred. However, the reference to the belief that an angel disturbed the water found in John 5:3b-4 is not found in the oldest manuscripts.

The pool continued to be known and revered for several centuries after New Testament times.

In fact, a Greek inscription has been found that commemorates a gift by a Roman lady, probably pagan. In the second century AD, Christians probably baptized in one or more of the pools. In the middle of the fifth century AD, Eudocia, widow of Emperor Valentinian III, built a church in the shape of a sailing ship along the porch dividing the two pools. Several centuries later, when this Byzantine structure lay in ruins, the Crusaders erected a church adjacent to the site of the pool. The Crusaders' structure is known as the Church of St. Anne. Saladin, twelfth-century sultan of Egypt, the Mohammedan commander who successfully opposed the crusade of Richard the Lion-Hearted, converted the Church of St. Anne into a school bearing his name.

The Pool of Bethesda today is on the property of the "White Fathers" who serve the Church of St. Anne, which still stands as a good example of Norman architecture.

The excavators who discovered the pool found it about twenty feet below present ground level. Excavations have continued and a considerable amount of the complex now can be seen.

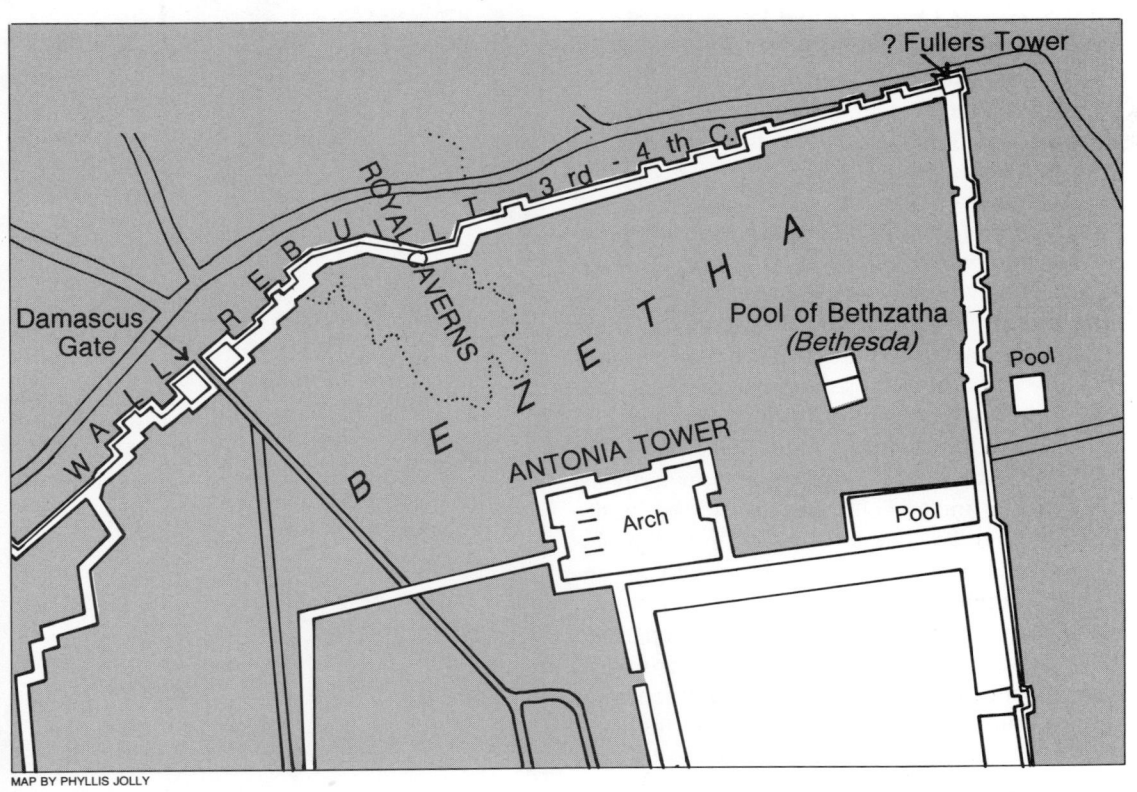

MAP BY PHYLLIS JOLLY

The Gihon Spring and the Pool of Siloam

Rice A. Pierce

"[Jesus] said unto him, Go, wash in the pool of Siloam" (John 9:7).

What was so important about "the pool of Siloam"? Of course we know that it was *Jesus*, not the waters of the pool, who healed the man who had been blind from birth. Yet the Pool of Siloam was important to the people of Jerusalem in Jesus' day—and for centuries before that time.

A source of water was critical to the earliest inhabitants of Jerusalem. The only natural spring in the immediate vicinity was Gihon (1 Kings 1:33). When the dry season lasted many months and the rainy season only a few, this gushing natural spring formed the center of early Israel's life. In fact, the first settlement there on the Ophel hill occurred just above this spring.

"Gihon" (the Hebrew name *giha* means "a gushing forth") was a spring in the northeast part of the ancient city area (southeast of the present city). Its waters increased their flow intermittently. This gushing was caused by an unusual siphoning action of underground caverns. Each gush lasted about forty minutes, separated by a period of some seven hours according to the season. Gihon's waters served for centuries as the chief source of drinking water and the city's irrigation. The spring was always located outside the city walls.

Ancient Gihon Spring tunnel, looking back toward entrance.

ILLUSTRATOR PHOTO/DAVID ROGERS

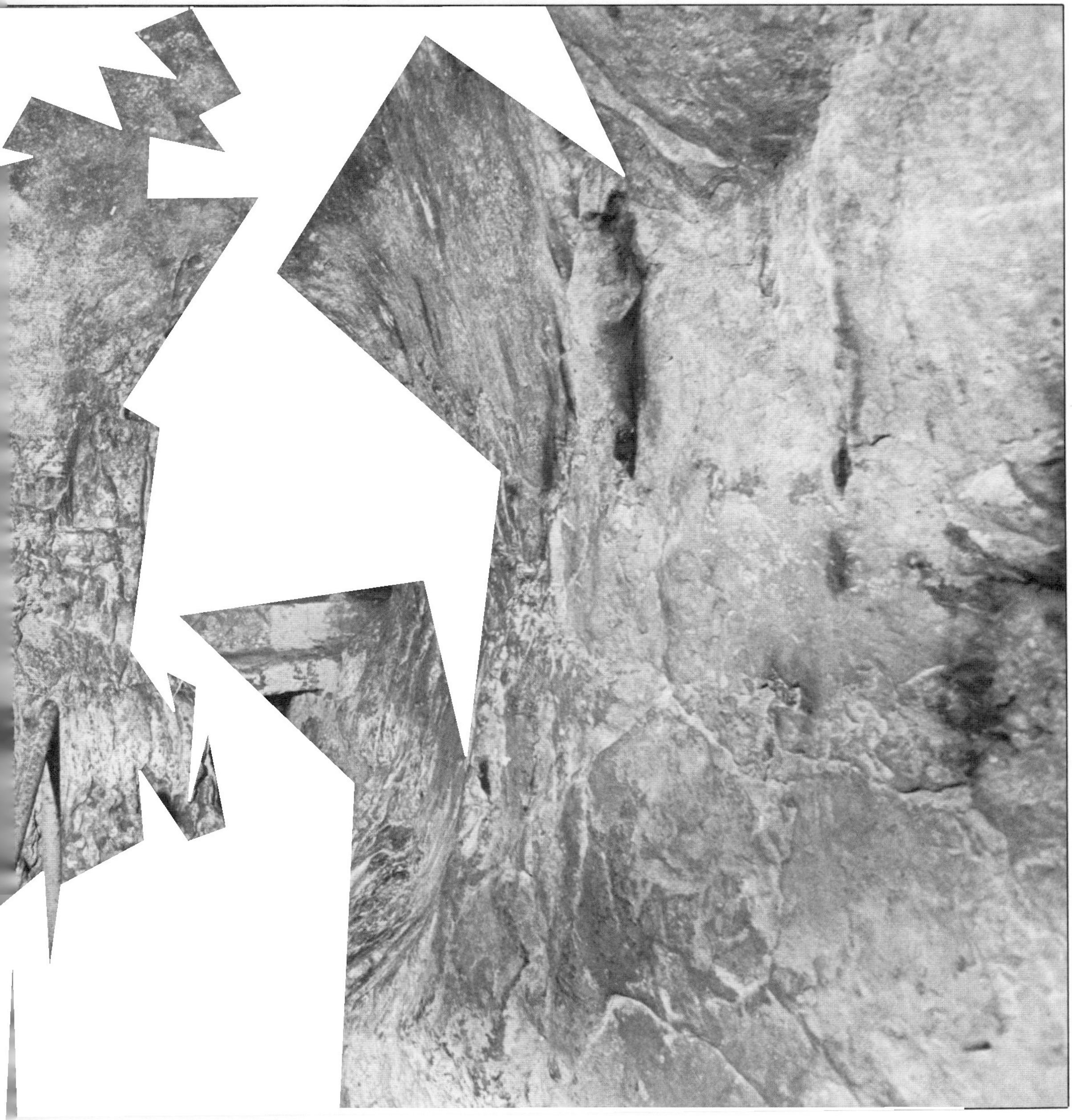

ILLUSTRATOR PHOTO/DAVID ROGERS

The walkway inside the Gihon tunnel (above) is short; the rest of the journey must be by wading. *Right:* Stairway from Gihon entrance.

The Jebusites, the inhabitants of the holy mount prior to the Conquest, constructed a finely conceived way of bringing water from the spring into the city. Moving from the spring into the city, the conduit was made up of (1) a horizontal channel leading from the spring; (2) a vertical shaft going up to a platform some forty feet from the channel; and (3) a stepped tunnel leading from the platform where the water was drawn to the city inside the wall. From inside the city walls, persons walked down and through the tunnel, used buckets to draw up water from the channel through the shaft, and returned to the tunnel exit within the city wall. The tunnel was chiefly defensive in purpose. Likely it was through this secret shaft and tunnel that Joab was able to penetrate the city's defenses for David (2 Sam. 5:8).

David occupied and extended the walls of the city. The Israelites then built an open-air trench to carry water from the Gihon pool in the north (later called the "upper pool") all the way to the south of the city, forming a reservoir later called the "lower pool." Since this trench was exposed to enemy control, another trench was built, possibly by David or Solomon, closer to the city walls. This possibly was the stream to which Isaiah alluded ("the waters of Shiloah that go softly," 8:6).

Thus were the precious spring waters of Gihon being used when Hezekiah became king of Israel. Because of his acts of independence while a vassal of the Assyrian Sennacherib, invasion threatened. With great energy Hezekiah reinforced the walls of the city. Then he turned his attention to the water supply—the other vital concern for survival in those times. The spring and aqueduct were quite open to the enemy, who could both use the water supply and cut it off from Jerusalem. Hezekiah set about to remedy the problem as he called his council together (2 Chron. 32:3-4). When he and his people had finished the task, they had accomplished one of the great engineering feats of ancient history.

Hezekiah constructed a tunnel through the Ophel hill from the Gihon spring northeast of the city. It moved under the wall and surfaced at a spot within the walls in the southwest of the city (2 Chron. 32:30). This latter place where the water emptied came to be known as the Pool of Siloam. With the spring walled off from the enemy, fresh water came through the new tunnel to Israel's people and army. They withstood the siege of Sennacherib.

Some scholars believe the pool originally was roofed over like a cistern. Its overflow ran through an enclosed channel and emerged outside the walls to water the king's gardens. The ceiling, if there ever was one, collapsed sometime later and the pool was made open. The stones that appear today are Roman.

The history of the tunnel, spring, and pool had only begun. Sennacherib invaded Palestine and threatened Jerusalem in 701 BC. Hezekiah's tunnel was completed about 702 BC. The tunnel still was known by Jewish writers in the second century BC, yet in the first century AD the Jewish historian Josephus apparently knew nothing of it. He assumed that Siloam's waters came into the pool from a spring at the spot. He referred to the "fountain" of Siloam in his detailed description of Jerusalem. The tunnel by this time no doubt had begun to fill with calcium carbonate deposits.

The tunnel that connected the Pool of Siloam and the Gihon Spring apparently first was rediscovered in the thirteenth century. Not until the nineteenth century, however, was its existence generally known. Siloam's tunnel from Gihon was first explored by the American biblical scholar, Edward Robinson. With a missionary friend, Eli Smith, he traveled the whole length of the tunnel in April, 1838.

While making the 1,749-foot underground journey, the two men made a startling discovery as to the tunnel's route. The course of the conduit makes a long *S*. Theories vary as to why the route wound in such fashion. Some scholars think Hezekiah charged the diggers with avoiding the tombs of the Davidic kings. Others think the workers simply sought the easiest way through the softer rock formations. Still others think the route of an ancient underground stream, by that time dried up, was followed for ventilation purposes. A fourth group thinks the calculations simply may have been primitive.

Nevertheless, the tunnel came into being: some 1,749 feet long, 6 feet high, 2 feet wide. It took 6 to 7 months to dig it.

First, however, let us recognize the great work which English Captain Charles Warren did in exploring the Pool of Siloam's source, the Gihon Spring, in December, 1867. Warren observed the tunnel leading from the spring. Looking closely, he saw a cavity in the roof. Having been an Alpine climber, he secured ropes and a ladder and explored the cavity. Soon he discovered that the cavity was the bottom of a shaft leading from the tunnel through the Ophel rock into the city. Warren had discovered the defensive water system the ancient Jebusites had used throughout the period of the judges! It likely was the route Joab had used to get into the fortress-city for David.

In June 1880 a remarkable event occurred regarding the Pool of Siloam. The event was an "accident," a way in which some of the world's most valuable discoveries have been made. A pupil of Conrad Schick, German architect and engineer of Jerusalem, was playing in the Siloam tunnel with some friends. His foot slipped and he fell into the pool. As he got up he noticed some marks on the wall which he fingered and thought looked like unusual writing. The boys reported to Schick what they had

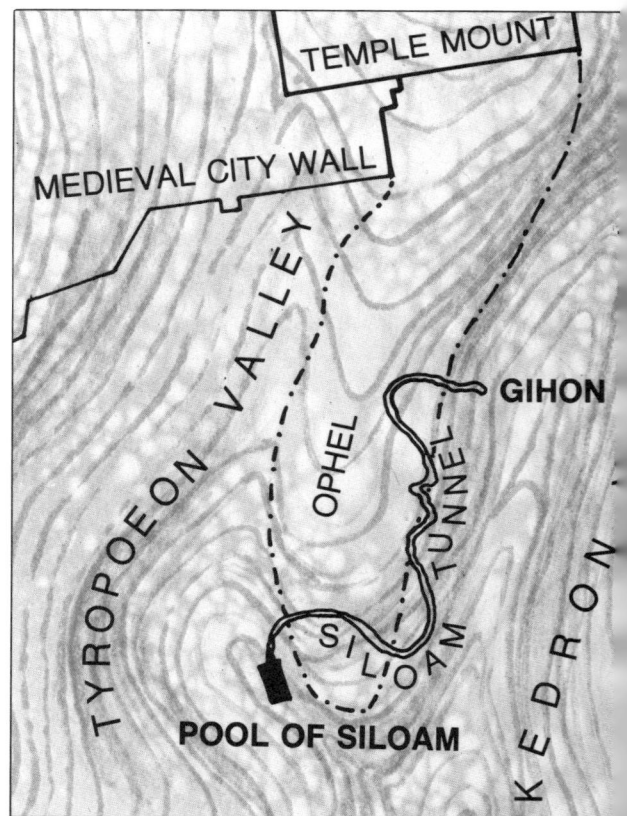

MAP BY PHYLLIS JOLLY

seen. Schick soon discovered that the writing indeed was unusual! It was fine classical Hebrew, the oldest known Hebrew inscription of any length then known. And of much additional significance, the inscription had been written in 700 BC, possibly by a worker, to record the completion of Hezekiah's tunnel. It reads: "[. . .] the breakthrough. Now this is the manner of the breakthrough. While still [. . .] the axe, each toward his fellow, and while three cubits still remained to be tunnel[led], the voice of a man [was hea]rd calling to his fellow, for there was a fissure (?) in the rock on the right [. . .] Now when the tunnel was cut through, each of the excavators hewed through to meet his fellow, axe against axe, and the waters began flowing from the source toward the reservoir for 1200 cubits, 100 cubits being the height of the rock above the heads of the excavators."

ernment to Turkey to prepare for the Chicago Exhibition of 1893. While visiting Jerusalem he called on a Greek, who was away from home for the moment. His wife showed Dr. Adler some antiquities in their home. To Adler's great surprise, the rock-cut Siloam inscription was among them! Apparently the Greek had had the inscription cut out of the tunnel wall, with the connivance of the authorities, and was in negotiation with foreign museums for its sale. Adler contacted Peters, who was in Constantinople. Peters contacted the imperial Turkish government. The Turkish governor of Jerusalem was ordered to reclaim the tablet, which he did. Peters had the honor of lifting the heavy inscription and putting it in place in the Museum of the ancient Orient, Constantinople (now Istanbul). It may be seen there today. (Peters says that while he was in Jerusalem in 1920, the Zionist

MATSON

The Siloam Inscription, found where tunnel diggers met.

Despite the fact that the first part of the inscription apparently is missing, here is a remarkable discovery for studying the development of the Hebrew language. The half-a-year's labor, with men digging from each end, had ended finally on a triumphant note. And the discovery caused the same kind of tremendous excitement in the world of biblical scholarship.

In 1890 vandals removed the Siloam inscription from the tunnel wall. John P. Peters tells in intriguing fashion[1] how the stolen inscription tablet was discovered by chance in Jerusalem. Cyrus Adler, an American, was sent by his gov-

authorities asked him if he would cooperate to relocate the stone again in Jerusalem. Peters wrote that he thought this would be done, but it was not.)

The story of the Pool of Siloam would not be complete, even in this brief fashion, without paying tribute to the work of Captain Montague

ILLUSTRATOR PHOTO/DAVID ROGERS

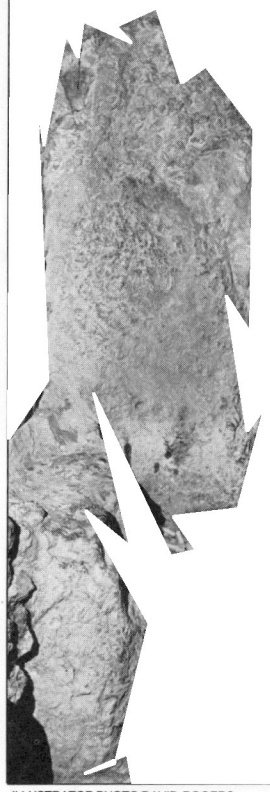

Opposite: Siloam opening where Gihon empties into pool. *Left:* Inside of tunnel near Siloam pool. *Below:* Overflow side of Siloam pool.

ILLUSTRATOR PHOTO/DAVID ROGERS

ILLUSTRATOR PHOTO/DAVID ROGERS

Parker. With a staff of British engineers and sound financial backing, in 1909 Parker thoroughly excavated, explored, surveyed, and measured the Siloam tunnel and pool. They cleaned out the tunnel and restored it to its original width and height. The total fall in elevation from the Gihon spring to the Pool of Siloam was found to be seven feet, two inches. At the point of breakthrough for the tunnelers, 944 feet from the Siloam end, the floor of the southern half was only one foot higher than the northern half!

Today the Pool of Siloam is largely unused as a reservoir. The water is brackish, but the whole system could be restored with water from the modern Gihon. (The present pool is of more recent construction than the one in Jesus' time, but the location is about the same.) The modern village of Silwan encompasses the pool area today, but there seems to be no connection between Silwan and the New Testament.

One may walk easily through the Siloam tunnel today. And because of recent discoveries the visitor may descend, from the outside, the very steps Jesus probably used prior to his arrest. They lead down into the Tyropoeon Valley and toward the Pool of Siloam. The construction of a church in the fifth century greatly altered the tunnel exit into the pool. Later a mosque was erected over the ruins of the church. Today a small minaret stands over the remaining part of the pool.

[1] John P. Peters, *Bible and Spade* (New York: Charles Scribner's Sons, 1922), pp. 174-75.

ILLUSTRATOR PHOTO/KEN TOUCHTON

Lazarus' Tomb

Joe O. Lewis

Lazarus' tomb lies just beyond the Mount of Olives from Jerusalem. It wasn't a long walk in Jesus' time, but for those of us who are not used to walking great distances, the long uphill climb of more than a mile would be a challenge. The Christian who goes to Lazarus' tomb now approaches by bus or car from Jerusalem. The road leaves the Old City and goes across the Kidron Valley, passing the Mount of Olives and the church marking Gethsemane. Then the road bends upward over the Mount of Olives (see photo 6, p. 69) and, after affording a look back at the magnificent panorama of the Temple Mount with its Dome of the Rock, it leads to the village of el-Azariyeh.

The village of el-Azariyeh is the site of ancient Bethany. Modern archeological excavation has shown that the original town was a few hundred yards closer to the top of the Mount of Olives, but there is little doubt that the present village is the descendant of the earlier city. The Arabs call their town el-Azariyeh after Lazarus. Some Moslems have called the village el-Eizariyeh in memory of Ezra who brought the law back from the Babylonian Exile, according to Saller, one of the better sources on this subject.[1] This confusion may have arisen because of a legend that Ezra also was raised from the dead to bring back the law.

While the buildings there now do not date from Jesus' time, they are built from the same white stone used then and differ mostly in size and number. When Jesus stayed in the home of Mary, Martha, and Lazarus in Bethany the village was a quiet suburb of Jerusalem. Bethany is mentioned once in the Old Testament; at least

ILLUSTRATOR PHOTO/KEN TOUCHTON

Entrance (left) and stairs (right) to Lazarus' tomb likely were cut in the 16th century, but the tomb must be authentic.

most scholars seem to agree that the Ananiah of Nehemiah 11:32 is the same Bethany. The late W. F. Albright, a well-known biblical archeologist, established the identification of the two sites as early as 1924.

After the New Testament period, Bethany came to be identified with Lazarus. One of the earliest travelers to write about this tomb there was a woman named Aetheria. She gave a good description of the scene and described the worship ritual that was conducted at Bethany, which she called the Lazarium. When she arrived there in AD 395, it was customary to gather at the Lazarium on the Saturday before Palm Sunday to sing and read a worship service, which ended with the priest announcing the coming of Easter the next week. This was done because Jesus came to Bethany six days before Passover, according to the Gospel of John.

In the early 1950s a Franciscan archeologist, Father Sylvester J. Saller, excavated at Bethany. He discovered a series of churches built on the site of the tomb, the old city of Bethany a little distance away, and an area of tombs associated with that town. He concluded on the basis of written accounts about the churches that the earliest church had to date about AD 390 or slightly earlier. This church faced east and nearly joined the tomb of Lazarus at its western end. There was a small atrium or courtyard between the two. The fourth-century church was destroyed by an earthquake but the church was rebuilt a few yards farther east. In the twelfth century the church was altered and reconstructed once again. At that time a convent was built on the south side of the church and the tomb.

Interior of Lazarus' Tomb, with burial niches on sides. Tomb is attested very early in Christian history.

ILLUSTRATOR PHOTO/KEN TOUCHTON

> Death is swallowed up in victory.
> O Death, where is thy sting?
> O grave, where is thy victory?
>
> The glory of God shall be seen by those who put
> their faith in Jesus in times of greatest distress and
> hopelessness. They are certain that He is greater
> than any distress, even greater than Death itself.
>
> Der Tod ist verschlungen in den Sieg.
> Tod, wo ist dein Stachel?
> Hölle, wo ist dein Sieg?
>
> Herrlichkeiten Gottes sollen jene sehen,
> die in grösster Not und Auswegslosigkeit Jesus
> Glauben schenken, jenen, dass Er immer
> grösser ist als jede Not, selbst grösser als der Tod.

Bethany today, where excavations revealed occupation from 6th century BC. Finds include coins of Herod the Great and Pilate.

ILLUSTRATOR PHOTO/KEN TOUCHTON

The Moslems took over this territory, and in the sixteenth century they blocked up the entrance that led from the rear of the early church to the tomb of Lazarus. At that time Christians cut a new set of steps into the tomb from the north. This is the entrance used by pilgrims and tourists today when they walk up the steep rocky street and file down into the tomb. These steps likely were cut between 1566 and 1575. There now are twenty-two narrow and uneven steps which enter the tomb or, to be more accurate, the vestibule of the tomb. Two more steps lead into a passageway to the tomb's chamber. The tomb itself is about seven feet by eight feet and tall enough to stand in.

The interior of the tomb appears to today's visitor simply to be a small room with smooth walls. However, in 1906 a close examination of this tomb by F. Fenner was published which showed that behind the present walls were niches on three sides where bodies would have lain. Thus, the tomb was similar in design to several others found in the area by the excavator. In John 11:38 the tomb is called a cave (Greek: *spelaion*). The term *spelaion* means that the tomb was a vertical shaft with a room at the bottom rather than a horizontal opening which the average reader might normally assume. This information helps to clarify John's meaning of "a stone lay upon it." This tomb was not sealed by the round stone rolled in front of the door as was the tomb of Jesus (Luke 24:2). Instead, it had a stone laid across the shaft which led down into the tomb.

The vertical shaft usually led downward to a small room which either had recessed shelves cut into the wall or a rock bench around the wall. In Lazarus' tomb the grave seems to have had three shelves cut into the rock with an arch carved over each one. A similar kind of tomb construction was used in many tombs in the Jerusalem area about this same time. In such a tomb three bodies could be accommodated at once. If more burials were required the bones of the earlier burials were removed and placed in small stone chests called ossuaries.

In 1856 Edward Robinson wrote concerning the tomb that not even the slightest probability existed of its ever having been the tomb of Lazarus. One does not have to travel long in Israel today to realize the rather weak links some supposedly sacred sites have with the original events. However, there is literary evidence from AD 333 that shows that the present tomb has been associated with Lazarus at least since that time. Saller's archeological excavation has shown an unbroken sequence of churches built at this site, confirming the importance of the location in a dramatic fashion. It is certain that the tomb does not *look* like it did in Jesus' time. The many different descriptions given by its visitors make this clear by their differing and sometimes contradictory scenarios. In addition, the presence of many other tombs in the area makes confusion of grave sites entirely possible. But granting these factors, one can still feel confident of being on or very close to sacred ground when he visits the tomb of Lazarus in Bethany.

---

[1]Sylvester J. Saller, *Excavations at Bethany (1949-1953)* (Jerusalem: Franciscan Press, 1957), p. 379.

New Testament Jericho

A. O. Collins

"But it's such a narrow road, and the place is not easy to get to . . . I'd rather not go," the guide protested, as I kept insisting that he take me to New Testament Jericho. Finally, when he agreed, we left the main highway and followed a rocky road westward for less than a mile to Tulul Abu el-Alayiq. Undisturbed by the hordes on the regular Jericho tours, we could survey the ruins of Herod's winter capital.

Throughout history, several sites have borne the name of Jericho. In the period of the Hasmoneans and the Herods, a second city arose to the south. By the Byzantine period (that began AD 334), still a third city of Jericho was built about a mile or so eastward.

The Wadi Kelt, a small stream fed by major perennial springs, served as the major water supply for the southern Jericho plain. In the layout of Herodian Jericho, buildings on both the north and south banks were oriented toward the Kelt streambed.

In Jesus' day, Jericho was a prominent city of Judea, strategically located on the route from Galilee to Jerusalem. To avoid the contamination of going through Samaria, Galilean pilgrims to the Jewish feasts crossed the Jordan River, traveled down the eastern side of the valley, forded the river near Jericho, then passed through the frontier city before they climbed the treacherous road to Jerusalem.

Early historical records attest to the economic significance of the Jericho Valley (see photo 19, p. 106), known for its quality dates and various medicinal plants, particularly balsam, which grew only in that locality. Josephus commended the palm trees as numerous and excellent (*Antiq.* XV. iv. 2). In the apocryphal work

Roman bridge on Jericho to Jerusalem road. Many priests lived in Jericho, and Herod had a winter palace there.

Sycamore trees in Jericho of the sort Zacchaeus climbed.

Ecclesiasticus, in proclaiming her greatness, Wisdom compares herself to the proverbially lush rose plants of Jericho (24:14). Antony presented Cleopatra with the revenues from the rich plantations of Jericho (Josephus *Antiq.* XV. iv. 2); Strabo, the Greek geographer, stated that the revenues from the grooves around Jericho were tremendous (*Geography* XVI. 2. 41). Because all merchandise that entered the city was subject to custom duties, the assignment as tax collector in Jericho was highly remunerative. It is not surprising that the publican Zacchaeus was so wealthy (Luke 19:2).

Throughout antiquity, military fortresses were established at or near Jericho because of its strategic location. Jericho served as district headquarters for the Persians, and the pattern was continued by subsequent rulers. During the Maccabean revolt, fortifications in the Jericho area were erected by the Syrian general, Bacchides (1 Macc. 9:50). At the military stronghold of Doq, near Jericho, Ptolemy murdered Simon the Hasmonean and his sons (134 BC; 1 Macc. 16:11-17).

In 63 BC, the Roman general Pompey, while clearing the Jericho area of robber hideouts, encamped near Jericho for one night and destroyed the forts of Threx and Taurus that commanded approaches to the city (Strabo *Geography* XVI. 2. 40). Gabinius made Jericho a council seat when he reorganized Judea into five districts (58 BC; Josephus *Wars* I. viii. 5).

On his march southward in AD 68, toward the defeat of Jerusalem, Vespasian established a garrison at Jericho. Josephus is not clear as to Jericho's eventual fate, but both Eusebius and Jerome state that the city was destroyed during the Jewish wars (AD 66-70). By AD 70, the city had lost its economic and military importance and became little more than a garrison town, never to achieve real significance again. In the fourth century, the city was replaced by Eriha (Erikha), the Byzantine settlement on the irrigated plain to the east, over which the present city has been built.

Though the excavations at Tulul Abu el-Alayiq, the site of New Testament Jericho, have revealed pottery remains from the Chalcolithic

Location of New Testament Jericho

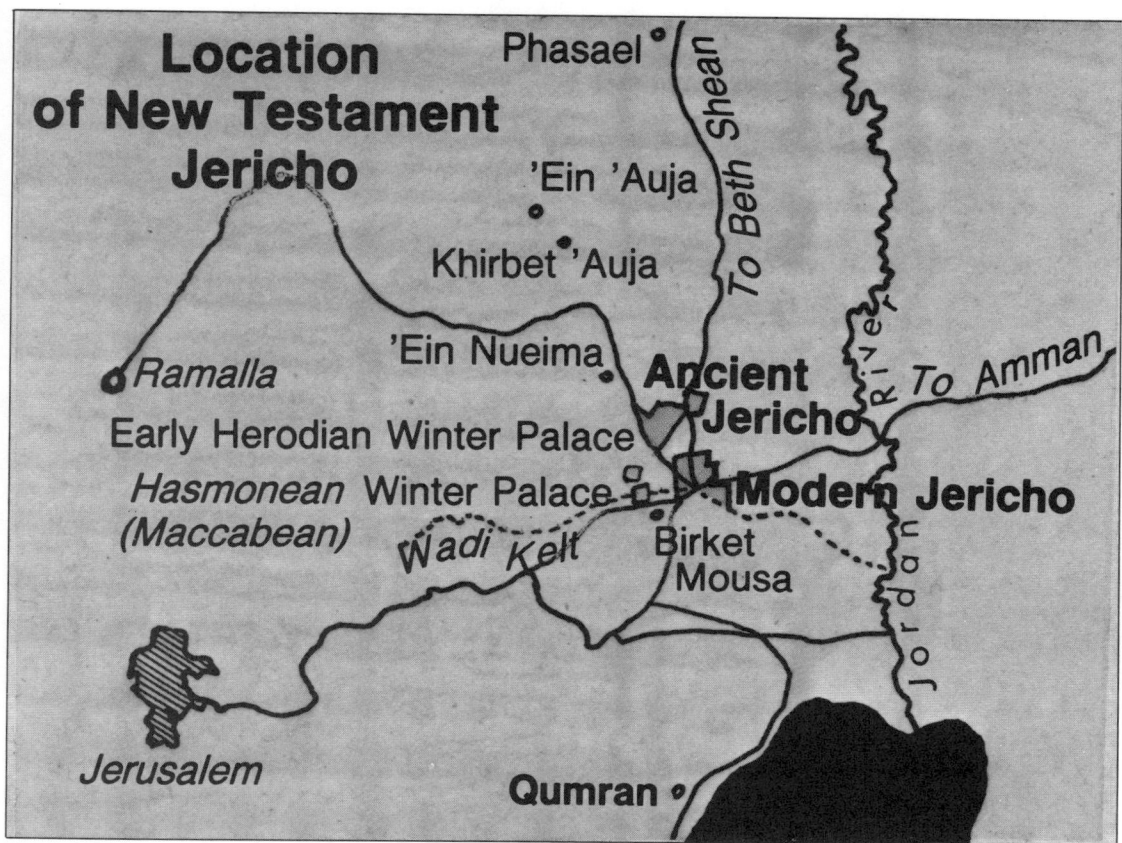

MAP BY PHYLLIS JOLLY

(4500-3000 BC) and Early Bronze Ages (3000-2100 BC), no definite conclusions can be made as to the extent of settlement in those periods. Of special concern is the material relating to the time of the Hasmoneans and Herods.

North of the Wadi Kelt, on a tell (Area A) which had attracted attention for decades, remains have been found of a Hasmonean palace (A1) that measured about 150 by 150 feet. In some places, two stories still are intact. The palace appears to have had a large central court surrounded by rooms of decorative plaster.

Aqueducts brought water to a nearby swimming pool (A3) that measured about 100 by 60 feet and which had steps leading to the bottom on each side. A broad ramp, about eighteen feet wide and half as deep as the pool, subdivided it into two parts. Consequently, when partially filled, the pool functioned as two shallow pools. In the court near the pool was found a hoard of coins that date from the time of Antigonus, the last Hasmonean king (40-37 BC). Possibly in this palace Alexandra entertained Herod as guest during the Feast of Tabernacles (36 BC); and in this very pool Herod had his brother-in-law, Aristobulus, drowned (Josephus *Antiq.* XV. iii. 3). South of the pool was a building about 60 by 50 feet that probably served as a poolside pavilion.

Probably one of the most prolific builders of all time, Herod the Great, found Jericho an ideal location for his winter capital. Its mild climate in winter appealed to government officials and religious leaders alike. Talmudic sources (Taanit 27; 67; Pesahim 4:30) reveal that many priests

Sites of New Testament Jericho

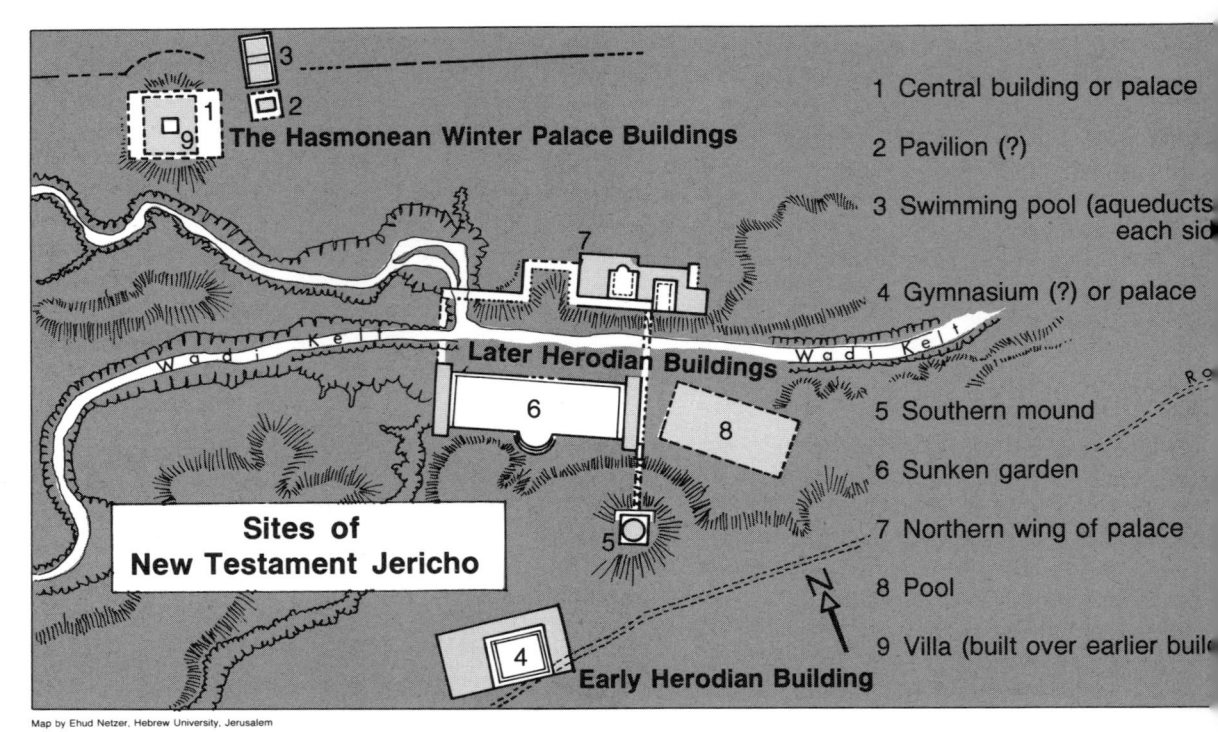

The Hasmonean Winter Palace Buildings
Later Herodian Buildings
Early Herodian Building

1 Central building or palace
2 Pavilion (?)
3 Swimming pool (aqueducts each sid[e])
4 Gymnasium (?) or palace
5 Southern mound
6 Sunken garden
7 Northern wing of palace
8 Pool
9 Villa (built over earlier buil[ding])

Map by Ehud Netzer, Hebrew University, Jerusalem

and Levites lived in Jericho; the probable ratio was one Jerusalem resident to two residents outside of Jerusalem, most of whom lived in Jericho. Priests leisurely enjoyed the semitropical Jordan Valley between their courses or rotation of service in the Temple. It is no coincidence that a Levite and priest were travelers along the Jericho road in Jesus' parable of the good Samaritan (Luke 10:25-37).

The first building constructed by Herod probably was a palace south of the Kelt, which Pritchard first labeled as a gymnasium (B4). Rectangular in plan, the structure included a large open central court, a six-room bathhouse, and a large hall with columns alongside.

Within the palace area was found a cache of 122 unguentaria, small vases which were ordinarily used for oils and spices. In the light of discoveries at Masada and Herodium, this building could have served as more than a gymnasium and more than likely was a residential palace. It is also likely that the pool located about 350 yards to the east, with the Arabic name *Birket Mousa* (C8), may have been built in the early part of Herod's reign.

Late in his reign, Herod conducted his most extensive project at Jericho. He incorporated the earlier structure (B4) into a larger complex which dominated both the north and south sides of the wadi. Similar to a modern "world's fair exposition grounds," the royal estate (Area C) was comprised of a southern artificial mound (C5), connected by a grand stairway to an exotic sunken garden and facade (C6), with a corresponding palace wing on the opposite bank of the stream (C7), all designed and built according to a master architectural plan.

Two building techniques were used in the expanded palace; conventional masonry characterized most of the enterprise. Yet, with a keen eye for beauty and style, Herod sought to copy Augustan architectural features that he had observed on Roman visits. A second kind of masonry known as *opus reticulatum* (a mortar-type of masonry, lined with small square-faced stones, and set at a 45 degree angle into the plaster to give the appearance of a net [hence its name]) had been introduced to Rome by Augustus; Herod's Jericho is the only place east of Italy where this feature is found extensively. Also, there was a characteristic *opus quadratum* (a type of stonework shaped like large bricks and laid at an angle) feature for corners, doorjams, etc. Other Roman features that Herod incorporated into his new palace are the niches and the sunken garden.

The southern mound offered a magnificent view in all directions, and there Herod constructed a square building (C5) that contained a round hall of Roman concrete, probably a reception hall. A steep stairway about 150 feet long descended from the north side of the mound to a stairwell in the buildings below, similar to a stairway that was discovered at Herodium. On the lower level, a spectacular facade that served two functions ran from east to west for about 360 feet. It formed the south side of a sunken garden and also was a retaining wall for gardens below. In the exact center of the facade was a hemicycle, a hemispheric structure with a stairway in the center. Low terraced walls ran up the slope, and flower pots, found *in situ* (in location) by the excavators, added to the terraced garden effect. The lowest point of the hemicycle had a water basin that, when uncovered, proved still to be watertight. Alternating semicircular and rectangular niches, possibly intended for statues, twenty-four on each side of the hemicycle.

Most of the actual palace was located north of the wadi. Though much material has washed away, recent excavations discovered two courts, a huge reception hall (the main unit of the wing), a smaller hall, a bathhouse, and many other rooms for storage and living (C7). The large hall was identical in plan with the earlier palace or "gymnasium" (B4), yet was over twice as large. The bathhouse had five rooms, built of Roman concrete and mudbrick, yet decorated with colored plaster. Rows of columns on the east and west added to the magnificence of the site, and a northern row of columns furnished a link between the northern complex and the sunken gardens across the riverbed.

On the northern artificial mound, remains were found of a building (A9), possibly a villa, that had been superimposed on the earlier Hasmonean building (A1). Ornamental gardens and bathing facilities had been added also in the later building enterprise.

In the recent explorations, no traces have been found of the palace burned by Simon the rebel, nor of the palace supposedly reconstructed by Archelaus. However, Netzer, while probing the horseshoe-shaped mound Tel el Samarat, theorizes that he may have located a structure that served as both theater and hippodrome.

Herod died in Jericho (4 BC). Anticipating his death, he moved to the comfort and warmth of the Jericho oasis. He ordered his son Antipater killed, made arrangements for the division of his territory, and then summoned his sister, Salome, and her husband, to give them final instructions. Since he feared that he would not be mourned adequately, Herod had imprisoned a large number of Jewish leaders in the Jericho hippodrome and commanded that at his death the men would be executed. That mass execution would ensure a shock wave of grief throughout the land. Through this scheme, the paranoid despot sought to accomplish two things: (1) to assure a proper amount of mourning, and (2) to rid the land of certain leaders. However, rather than follow Herod's wishes, Salome dismissed the prisoners, gathered the military leaders in the Jericho amphitheater, and asked them to follow their new king, Archelaus (Josephus *Antiq.* XVII. viii. 2).

The first excavation of New Testament Jericho was in 1868, when Sir Charles Warren sank shafts across the southern mound (Area C5); his conclusions were that his location of the site as Herod's city was in error. In 1909 and 1911, Ernst Sellin dug an exploratory trench in search of the Herodian ruins; he too failed to recognize the uniqueness of the site.

Not until 1950 was the next project at Tulul Abu el-Alayiq attempted, under the direction of James Kelso. The United Nations was considering damming the Wadi Kelt, and there was urgent need to determine what significant remains lay alongside the streambed. The expedition concentrated on ruins related to the south bank of the wadi (Area C), though some work was done on the north bank and the northern mound (Area A).

Excavation continued in 1951 under the leadership of James B. Pritchard. Southwest of the southern mound, an area was being used by local farmers to cultivate tomatoes (Area B). The field had a rectangular elevated section in the middle, with barren areas on the sides where plants grew poorly, which suggested that underlying walls might be there. The entire season was spent exposing this impressive building that Pritchard tentatively identified as a gymnasium.

Renewed excavations have been carried out since 1972 under the direction of Ehud Netzer of the Hebrew University of Jerusalem. First attention was focused on the northern mound (Area A) and the palace complex north of the wadi (Area C7). In the spring of 1975, the palace on the northern tell was excavated. Work continues periodically at the overall site.

As I walked among the Herodian Jericho ruins, my imagination reconstructed events from the life of Jesus. Though Jesus undoubtedly visited Jericho many times, his last visit especially stirred my imagination. En route to the Passover feast at Jerusalem, he encountered Bartimaeus and his friends (see Matt. 20:29-34; Mark 10:46-52; and Luke 18:35-43). Forbidden to work and ostracized by society, outcasts found the Jericho gate an advantageous place to beg. What better spot could blind men want? But Jesus, when he paused to hear them at the city's edge, gave them not only sight but salvation as well!

Herodian Jericho had public places where sycamore trees grew as high as fifty-five feet. Somewhere along this wadi, the curious little tax collector, Zacchaeus, had climbed to his sycamore perch in order to size up the Galilean rabbi.

ILLUSTRATOR PHOTO/KEN TOUCHTON

The tell of New Testament Jericho, seen from the Old Testament tell. The lush growth of modern Jericho lies beyond.

Then, as my visit to New Testament Jericho ended, I glanced westward and surveyed the Roman road that skirted the south side of the Wadi Kelt. Here Jesus bade farewell to Herod's city and climbed the heights to Jerusalem and crucifixion (see photo 47, p. 112).

It was time for me to leave Jericho as well. A few minutes later, at the traditional ruins of the Inn of the Good Samaritan, I looked westward and forward to catch my first glimpse of the Mount of Olives. As I looked back to the valley in the east, there stood Jericho: city of palms and balsam, winter capital of Herod, haven for beggars, and choice assignment for customs collectors—the last city our Savior visited before his final ordeal in Jerusalem.

Herod's Temple

William H. Stephens

Jesus' life and ministry, like that of any pious Jew, was intertwined with the Temple. His uncle Zechariah was a priest; he was presented there as an infant; he observed Passover there, taught and preached there, disputed with the religious authorities there; he paid the Temple tax; and his death caused the veil of the Temple to split.

Long before Jesus' day the Temple of Jerusalem had come to be the focal point of the Jewish faith. Herod's Temple was the third one built in Jerusalem. (Perhaps because Herod may have incorporated Zerubbabel's Temple into his own, Herod's is often referred to as the Second Temple.) Solomon's Temple may have been more elaborate than Herod's—we do not know for sure—but Herod's complex was much larger. It was, in fact, larger by far than any of the famous pagan temple centers, including Baalbek, Athens, and Rome.

Solomon evidently had leveled the Temple Mount for his structure. Herod took that platform and doubled its size. To do so, he had to divert the Tyropean Valley on the west and fill in the old bed; he also had to fill in the upper portion of the Kidron Valley on the east; and he had to extend the platform to the south (see photo 22, p. 106). The completed mount—a vast, flat courtyard now called the *Haram* (Arabic)—is 930 feet on the south, 1,050 feet on the north, 1,620 feet on the west, and 1,550 feet on the east, a total area of about 40 acres (the exact figures vary slightly in different sources).

This isometric drawing, done by Bill Latta from editor's specifications, shows the size and relationship of walls, courts, and the Temple proper.

DRAWING OF HEROD'S TEMPLE COMPLEX BY BILL LATTA

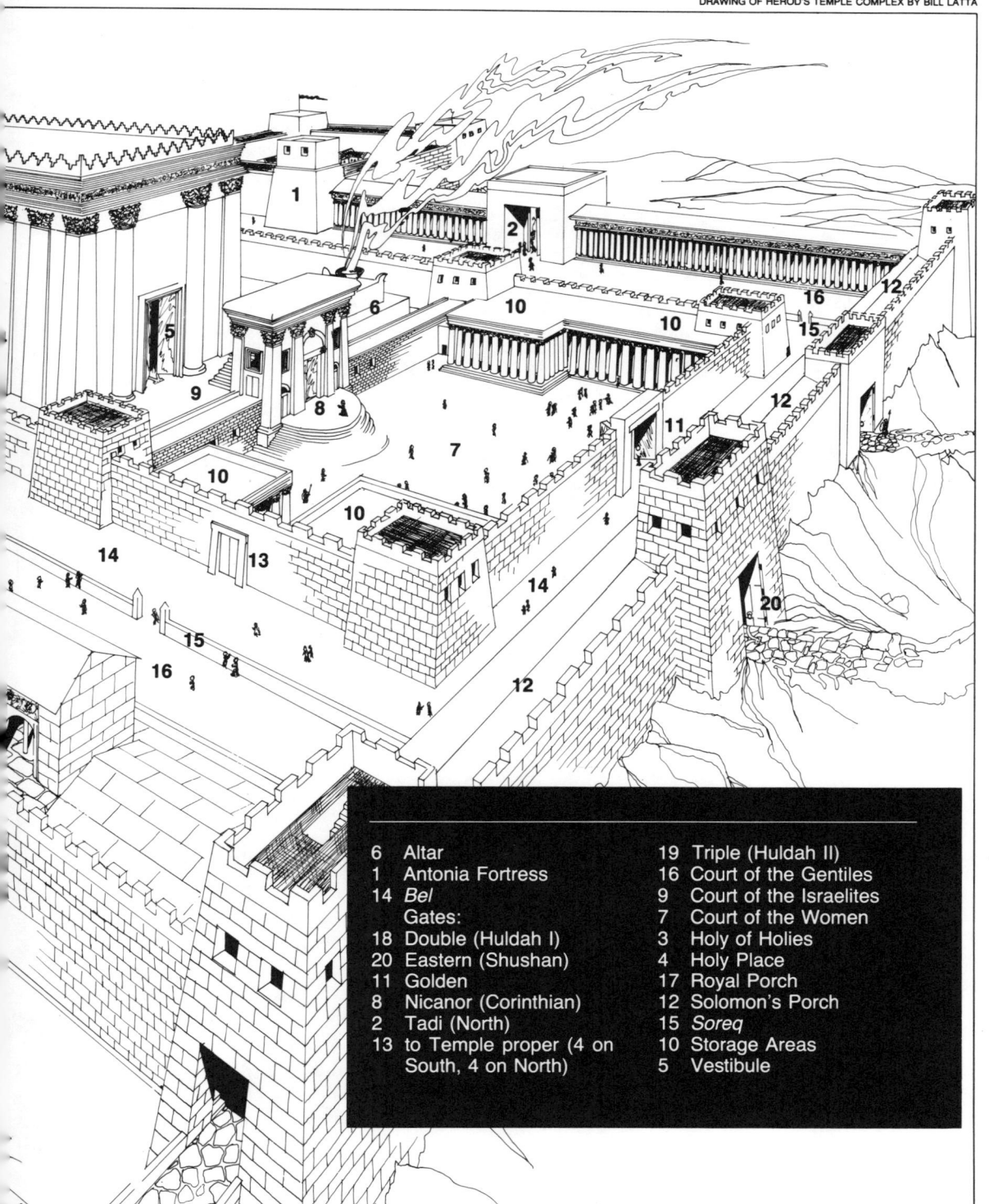

6	Altar	19	Triple (Huldah II)
1	Antonia Fortress	16	Court of the Gentiles
14	*Bel*	9	Court of the Israelites
	Gates:	7	Court of the Women
18	Double (Huldah I)	3	Holy of Holies
20	Eastern (Shushan)	4	Holy Place
11	Golden	17	Royal Porch
8	Nicanor (Corinthian)	12	Solomon's Porch
2	Tadi (North)	15	*Soreq*
13	to Temple proper (4 on South, 4 on North)	10	Storage Areas
		5	Vestibule

Below: From Jerusalem model, entrance from outside walls into court by Royal Porch. *Right top:* From model, Triple Gate on south wall. *Right, bottom:* Temple proper with Court of Gentiles surrounding.

ILLUSTRATOR PHOTO/KEN TOUCHTON

This energetic builder-king probably began construction about 20 BC. One thousand priests learned to be stonemasons so they could build the Temple proper while maintaining its ritual purity, and they completed their work in about eighteen months. The other main structures took about eight years to complete. However, the decoration and finishing continued until AD 64, more than thirty years after Jesus' crucifixion. At that time eight thousand men still were employed.

Except on the north side, where the approach to the mount was fairly level, the approaches were primarily uphill. The vulnerable north side was protected by the Fortress Antonia, which had been built on the foundations of an earlier protective fortress (variously called Tower of Hananel, Tower of the Hundred, and Baris). The Antonia was built on a precipitous rock about seventy-five feet high and covered with smooth flagstones. The fortress itself rose another sixty feet. Three of its four towers rose yet another seventy-five feet, while the fourth one at the southeast corner was some ninety-five feet high, from which the Temple area could be kept under watch. Steps led down into the Temple (Paul was saved from the mob by soldiers who quickly descended these steps), and a secret underground passage led to one of the inner eastern gates. Antonia was both a garrison and a palace. On the opposite side of the north wall was the massive Pool of Israel.

Broad porticoes encircled the Temple mount. The ones on the west, north, and east were forty-nine feet wide, consisting of double rows of marble columns running along a high wall. Each column towered about twenty-seven feet and was topped by a gold-leafed Corinthian capital (see photo 29, p. 110). The portico ceilings were of cedar. The eastern portico was called Solomon's Porch. The southern portico, called the Royal Porch, was more elaborate.

Jesus could have approached the Temple from any direction through several major gates: one on the north, five on the west, two on the south, and one on the east; small gates for special purposes also existed. Current excavations also have discovered numerous caverns, tun-

ILLUSTRATOR PHOTO/KEN TOUCHTON

ILLUSTRATOR PHOTO/KEN TOUCHTON

145

nels, and cisterns under the Temple Mount, used for various purposes. The best known of these is the so-called Solomon's Stables at the southeastern corner; they were built originally by Herod.

The entrances at the southern end probably were the most frequent approaches used by pilgrims. Ongoing excavations have established the design of this area in Jesus' day. From the south the pilgrim came to a broad paved plaza where he could mix with other pilgrims. An elevated street lay between the plaza and wide steps that led up to the southern gates. Shops were arranged under the roadway, and ritual baths were cut into the rock between two staircases so that pilgrims could purify themselves before entering the Temple area.

ILLUSTRATOR PHOTO/KEN TOUCHTON

Above: Southwest corner of Temple Mount showing Robinson's Arch and excavations. *Opposite:* Close-up of Robinson's Arch protrusion.

To go to the Temple mount from the south, Jesus would have climbed up 30 steps on a 215-foot-wide stairway to the Double Gates (Western Huldah Gate) or up a narrower stairway to the smaller Triple Gates (Eastern Huldah Gates). Once through the gates, Jesus would ascend an interior stairway to the mount, exiting in the massive Court of the Gentiles just beyond the Royal Porch.

All business connected with the Temple was conducted at the Temple, so the activity in the courtyard was bustling almost anytime, the feast days incredibly so. Rabbis and others taught and preached on the Torah in the porticos to groups large and small even as Jesus and his disciples did. The discussions from various meetings could be heard as one walked up and down the courtyard. In this court area, which surrounded the Temple proper, the changing of currency into the approved type, the purchase of sacrificial animals, and other business dealings were carried out.

The Royal Porch consisted of four rows of columns supporting a roof. Its southeast corner towered over the Kidron Valley, perhaps to a height of more than 150 feet, and generally is believed to be the pinnacle of the Temple. Numerous and varied activities were carried on in the Royal Porch, including business and meetings. The Sanhedrin had its home there beginning in about AD 30, very near the time of Jesus' crucifixion. At the opposite (western) end from the pinnacle, an entrance opened from a stairway that turned down into the Tyropean Valley to join the broad street that ran below the Temple Mount. A remaining stub of a support for this gate is called Robinson's Arch. The Kiphonos or West Gate, the remnants of which today are called Barclay's Gate, enters the western wall just up from Robinson's Arch. Jesus would have entered this gate at the lower street level, ascended up a passageway, and exited at the Temple Mount near the corner of the Western and Royal Porticoes.

The Temple area with its inner courts set about halfway between the southern and northern porticoes, about 150 yards from each one, and back to within some 50 feet of the Western

ILLUSTRATOR PHOTO/KEN TOUCHTON

ILLUSTRATOR PHOTO/KEN TOUCHTON

Porch. The Temple and its courts were separated from the Court of the Gentiles by the *soreq*. This balustrade was a latticed wall about 5 feet high that surrounded the Temple and its courts. It had a number of openings, beside each of which was posted a warning to Gentiles not to proceed further on penalty of death.

Two gates opened from the west right at the soreq—the one at its southwest corner (Wilson Arch) led from a massive stone bridge aqueduct that spanned the Tyropean Valley to connect with the Western Hill (Upper City) and Herod's palace; the other (Warren's Arch) led through a passageway from the street level to exit almost at the center of the back wall of the soreq. Another gate, about which little is known, entered farther north along the western wall. A large stretch of this western wall is the celebrated Wailing Wall—actually the foundation blocks for the Temple mount itself on which the walls were built.

To enter the Temple, Jesus would make his way across the varicolored paving stones of the court of the Gentiles and pass through the soreq. Once inside the balustrade he would ascend fourteen steps to a twenty-three-foot-wide platform, then climb five more steps to enter the inner court area through a gate on either the south, north, or east. (Three more gates each on the north and south led directly into the court of the priests.) All of the gates opened through massive but beautiful fortress walls some sixty-six feet high. All of the gates but one, the Nicanor Gate, were overlaid with gold and silver. Each of the three gates Jesus could enter led into the court of the women, located on the east side of the inner Temple complex.

The Temple faced east, so we would expect the east gates to be given special attention, and they were. The Golden Gate (see photo 30, p. 111) gave access from the Kidron Valley into the Court of the Gentiles. Also called the Eastern Gate or the Shushan (Persian) Gate, it was elaborately decorated. This gate has not been located by archeologists; the present Golden Gate is too far north and its construction is of too late a date to be the correct one. (Controversy exists concerning the identification of the Beautiful Gate, the Golden Gate, and the Nicanor Gate. The view presented here appears the most probable to this writer.)

ILLUSTRATOR PHOTO/DAVID ROGERS/ ARCHAEOLOGICAL MUSEUM, ANKARA

Opposite: Blocked-up portion of Double Gate (at inside corner) with monumental stairway at base of wall. *Above:* Warning Stone. *Below:* Closed-up Triple Gate on south wall.

ILLUSTRATOR PHOTO/KEN TOUCHTON

Jesus went through the Gate called Beautiful to enter the court of the women from the east. The court was not so named because only women could go there, but because women could go no farther. Actually, most of the religious celebrations except for those connected with sacrifice took place here, accented by the skill of the Levite musicians who played from the fifteen steps that ascended to the Nicanor Gate. Joyous celebration was common in the Court of the Women. A highlight of the year occurred when the high priest read the Torah on

ILLUSTRATOR PHOTO/KEN TOUCHTON

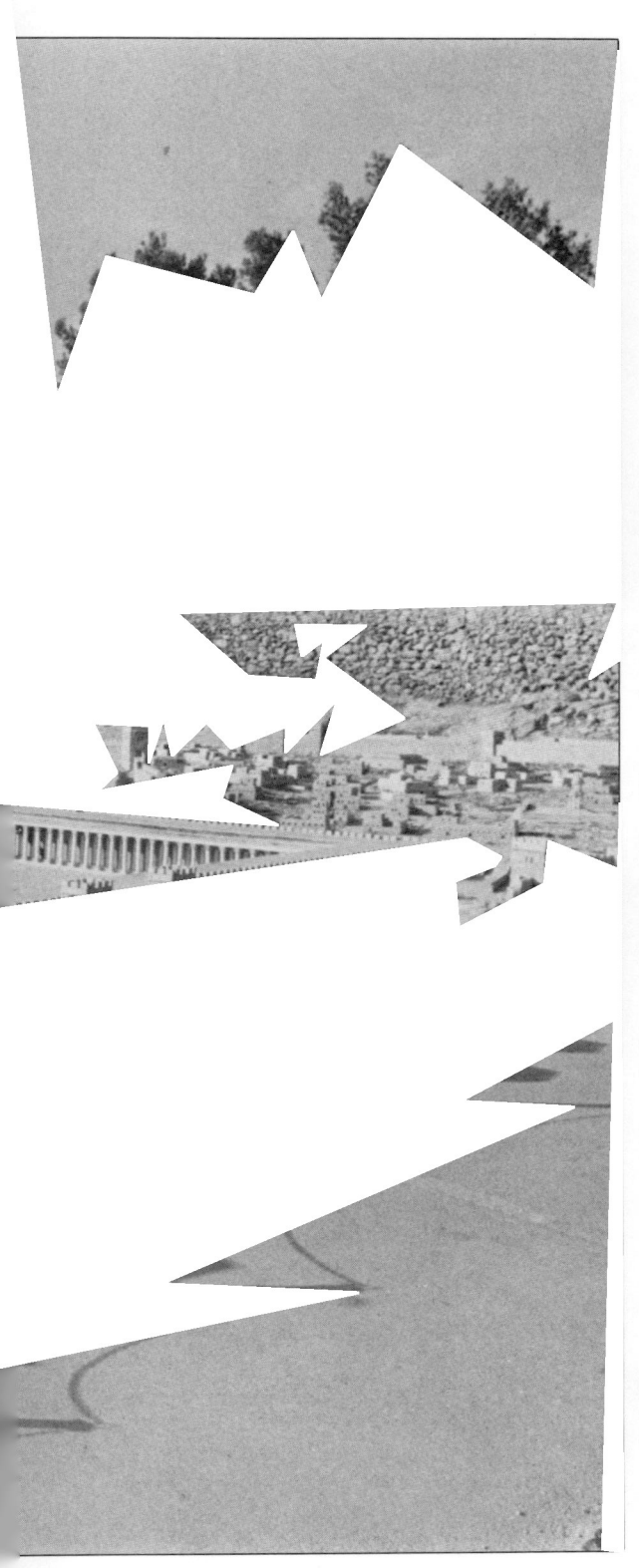

the Day of Atonement. The trumpet-like receptacles were located here to receive the offerings of silver shekels. The court would have been a large square except that rooms were built into each corner, each of which had its function for the Temple ritual: Chamber of Wood (northeast), Chamber of Nazirites (southeast), Chamber of Lepers (northwest), and Chamber of Oil (southwest). The fifteen steps from which the musicians played also had their more somber uses. Women who were suspected of adultery stood there to drink the "water of bitterness" (Num. 5:11-31). If they survived drinking it they were considered innocent—somewhat in the spirit of the medieval trial by combat. Or a woman might be made to climb up and down the stairs until she weakened enough to admit her guilt.

The Nicanor Gate was made of Corinthian bronze and far exceeded the other eight gates in value. It opened into the Court of the Israelites, an area eighteen feet or so wide where the men stood or prostrated and prayed while waiting their turn to sacrifice. Only ends of flagstones separated this court from the Court of the Priests, which surrounded the Temple proper and contained the altar. Laymen were required to participate in the slaughter and offering of sacrifices, and they went into the Court of the Priests only then or during the Feast of Tabernacles when they circled the altar caring palm branches. Levites sang from a nearby platform during the rituals.

Various chambers and rooms ran down both walls that flanked the inner court. The Chamber of Hewn Stone was situated to the left (south) of the Court of the Israelites. The Sanhedrin met here before they moved to the Royal Porch. Other chambers housed the rotating orders of priests when they served in the Temple, or served as storerooms for supplies.

Overview of Temple Mount (Jerusalem model) from southeast corner (Pinnacle); Lower City to left, Upper City beyond Mount; Bethesda (Bezetha) to right.

The entrance to the Temple proper is on a line with the Nicanor and the Beautiful Gates. The huge altar was in front of the entrance and a bit to the left. Priests climbed to the altar from a nonstaired ramp on its south side. The laver was between the ramp and the Temple. A slaughterhouse was situated to the right (north) of the altar. (Some authorities believe the altar was directly in front of the Temple entrance.)

When an Israelite offered his sacrifice, part of it was consumed by the fire and part was given either to the priest or taken back himself to be eaten, depending on the type of sacrifice. The priest's portion had to be cooked and eaten in the Court of the Priests. The layman's portion originally had to be cooked and eaten in the Temple area, as a family feast. However, as the crowds were so enormous, the Temple precincts were extended to include the older parts of the city. Pilgrims or residents could eat their sacrificial meals, then, in their lodgings, as Jesus and his disciples ate the Passover in the Upper Room.

The Temple proper, consisting of a porch, holy place, and holy of holies, was the focal point for all Judaism. The porch was thirty-five feet deep, seventy feet high, and may have extended well beyond the walls of the holy place on each side. Twelve steps led up to it from the Court of the Priests, further adding to its height. Heavily decorated, it contained two tables—one of marble, one of gold. The porch was enclosed except for a wide door covered with a heavy cloth decorated with stars. Massive walls that housed thirty-eight chambers connected at the back of the porch on each side and ran around the Temple.

The holy place was the primary place of priestly ritual. It was entered through golden doors. Daily ministrations were observed here within its gold-decorated walls. It contained the table (gold-plated) of shewbread, the gold incense altar and the seven-branched menorah (candlestick).

The holy of holies probably was higher than the holy place and was entered through the veil. Little is known about the curtain's arrangement. Some sources indicate two curtains, one extend-

ILLUSTRATOR PHOTO/KEN TOUCHTON

ing from each wall to meet in the center; others indicate a single curtain that opened from the bottom. At any rate, it hid the interior from view, for the inside of the holy place could be seen from the Nianor Gate. The holy of holies was completely empty, the ark and cherubim long since carried into foreign lands.

Scholars disagree as to where the Temple stood. The sacred rock Moriah, now covered by the golden Dome of the Rock (see photo 23, p. 107), is the focal point of the controversy. Called *es-Sakhra* now, the rock is about fifty-eight feet long, fifty-one feet wide, and from four to six-and-a-half feet high. Was the altar of Solomon's Temple built on the rock? Those who believe it was point out the channels cut into the stone, and the hole that corresponds to a chamber below. Was the holy of holies built over it? Those who hold this view claim that the Temple Mount in Solomon's day did not allow enough room west of the rock to build a temple. Further, the rock, being the highest point on the Mount, would be the place where the holiest part of the Temple would be built. This writer feels the latter view is more probable.

Jesus participated in all of the normal rituals and observances of Judaism. He sacrificed, and he surely walked every inch to which he had access on the Temple mount. None of the Temple buildings remain today; even the paving stones have been replaced. Excavations, though, have uncovered steps, doors, and passageways where Jesus walked. The Moslem buildings, of immense interest in their own right, do not keep the Christian from a sense of awe and piety, for the mount itself was a centerpiece of Jesus' life.

ILLUSTRATOR PHOTO/KEN TOUCHTON

Opposite: Nicanor (Beautiful) Gate, from model, was of solid bronze. *Right:* Dome of the Rock (right) and the silver dome of El Aqsa Mosque (left) seen from Mt. Scopus.

153

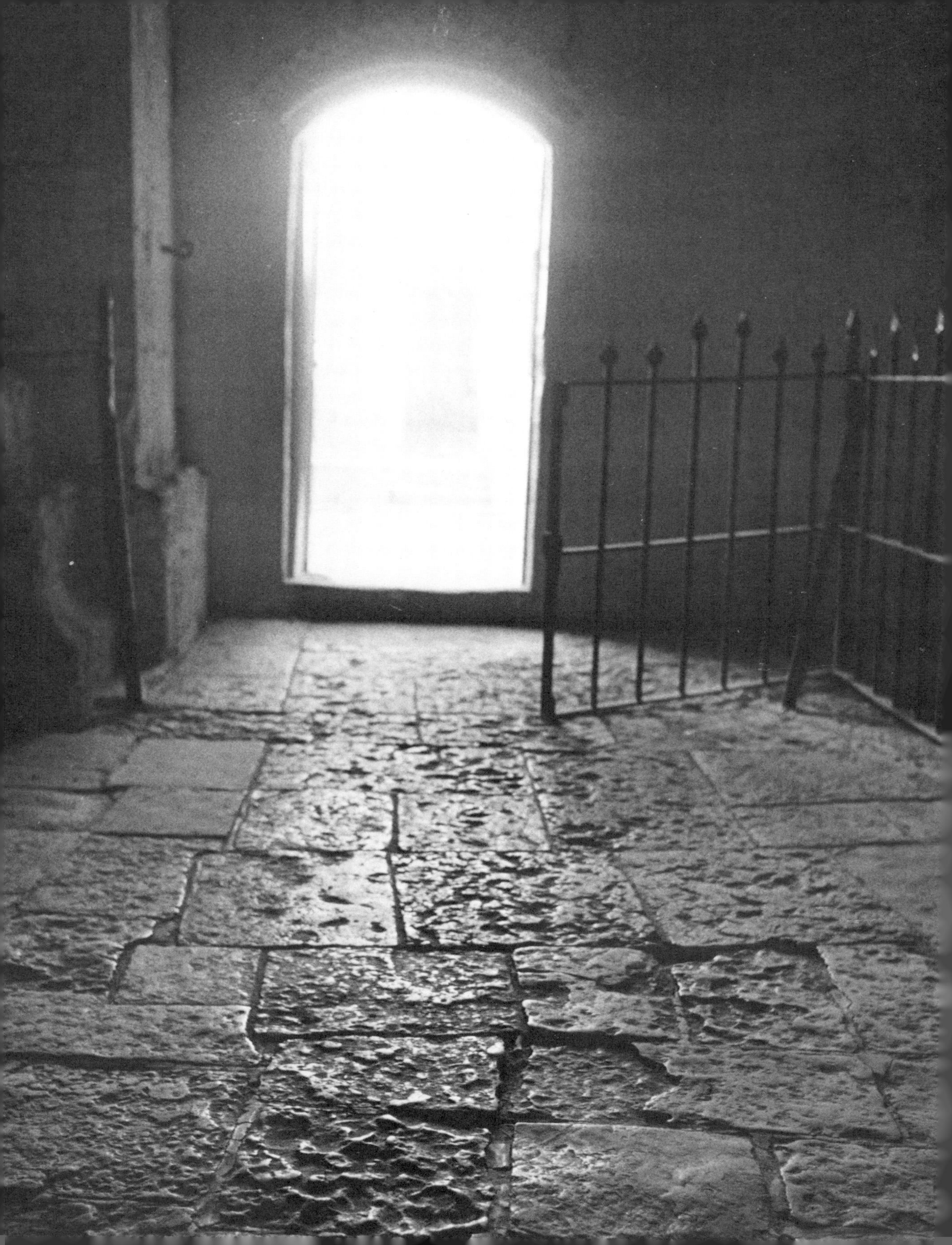

The Upper Room

Richard L. Williams

The first Lord's Supper took place during a meal among close friends in a private home. The location was chosen with precaution and deliberation by Christ himself so he could be alone with his disciples (see photo 26, p. 109).

The necessary arrangements to use someone's home were made in advance. When the proper time came, Jesus told Peter and John how they would locate the right place (Luke 22:8-12). While emphasis rightly has been focused on those present at the Lord's Supper and on what took place there, the location of this Upper Room has spurred considerable thought and curiosity as well.

The Upper Room, also known as the Cenacle (from a Latin word meaning "dining room"), was most likely on the second floor of someone's home in Jerusalem, perhaps that of John Mark's mother. If not a second-story room, it could have been a storage room or perhaps even a rooftop room like many Palestinian homes had in that day. Evidence favors the location as a guest room on the second floor, particularly as these were common in the city of Jerusalem (although not in the countryside).

Apart from the Synoptic accounts (Matthew, Mark, Luke), the Upper Room is only mentioned in Acts 1:13, though scholars are divided as to whether this last reference is to the same room. Acts 12:12 says that John Mark's mother allowed her home to be used for prayer, leading many to believe her home was used on both occasions, Passover and Pentecost.

The home that contained the Cenacle apparently survived the Jewish revolt in AD 68 and also the destruction of Jerusalem two years later. The area surrounding the Cenacle was least destroyed by the Romans in AD 70. The site lay outside the city walls. Epiphanius, a resident of Palestine who wrote in the fourth century, revealed that the Roman emperor Hadrian found the church with the upper chamber still stand-

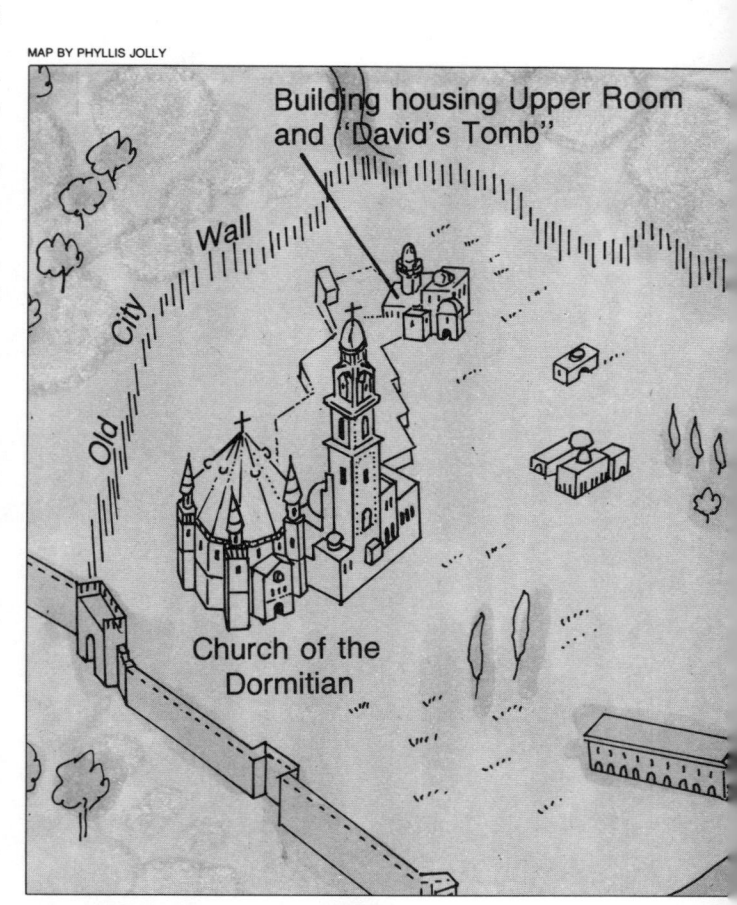

Opposite: Entrance to Upper Room, from inside.
Above, map: David's tomb, though revered, actually is on ruins of an ancient synagogue.

Below: Column from a 4th century Byzantine church on the site of the Upper Room. *Bottom:* Worn steps lead to Upper Room.

ILLUSTRATOR PHOTO/DAVID ROGERS

ILLUSTRATOR PHOTO/DAVID ROGERS

ing when he visited the city of Jerusalem in AD 135. This church was replaced by a larger one around 331-349. In 348 Cyril delivered a series of lectures in the Church of the Holy Sepulcher and talked of the Church of Sion. This church must have been the "Haghia Sion" (holy Zion), built larger and more splendid than the church Hadrian saw. A few years later the building was enlarged and beautified.

In AD 530 Theodosius described this church as the "mother of all churches." He believed that it was the house of John Mark's mother, located two hundred paces from the place where Jesus Christ died.

This church is included in the Madeba mosaic map. This important map of Jerusalem was built into the floor of a Byzantine church about AD 560, located today in Madeba, Jordan. The map has aided scholars considerably in their search for sites in Israel and Jerusalem.

A certain Arculf, a traveler in Jerusalem in AD 670, drew a sketch of the floor plan of the Zion Church. However, the earlier church was burned down in 614 by the Persians, so Arculf's church was a reconstruction. Once again, that building was destroyed.

The Cenacle shown today to tourists is a room on the second floor of a building erected in the fourteenth century by the Franciscans, next to the Church of the Dormition (sleep of death of Mary).

It measures approximately 50 feet, 2 inches by 30 feet, 10 inches. Three columns in a row divide the room into two areas (see photo). The entire complex of buildings has seen tragic fighting between Christians and Moslems but today is open to the public. The so-called tomb of David is nearby, down a flight of stairs.

While the present-day room obviously is not the original one, the evidence of tradition is strong enough and consistent enough to warrant a fair amount of confidence that when the Christian today stands in the upper room, he surely is very close to the room where the Last Supper took place.

Gethsemane and the Mount of Olives

Wayne Dehoney

The Mount of Olives is the most conspicuous landmark of the Jerusalem area. It is actually a mile-long limestone ridge interrupted by three summits. To the north is Mount Scopus, mentioned by the Jewish historian Josephus. Today the Hebrew University is located on the site. The road to the north from the Damascus Gate crosses Scopus and continues to Nablus (site of Jacob's well) and on into Samaria. The southern summit is the Mount of Offense (or Corruption). Here the foreign wives of Solomon erected altars to their pagan deities and worshiped their idols (2 Kings 23:13).

The central summit, rising 2,652 feet above sea level, is the Mount of Olives proper. From the crest of the mount one looks to the east across the barren, rolling, Judean wilderness to the Dead Sea. A very ancient road to Jericho skirts the base of the mountain and goes twisting into the Jordan valley to the southeast.

Facing in the opposite direction (to the west), one is overcome with an awe-inspiring sight. Below, at one's feet, lies the Kidron Valley. And across on the other side, rising in a magnificent panoramic display of grandeur and spreading across the hills of Zion, is Jerusalem (see panorame photos 27-29, p. 106).

This view of the Old City today is essentially the same view that overcame Jesus with emotion as he wept and foretold its destruction (Luke 19:41-44).

Both slopes of the Kidron Valley are covered with ancient and modern tombs—Jewish, Christian, and Moslem. Jews and Moslems alike have a strong desire to be buried on the slopes of this, the Valley of Jehoshaphat. Both groups, along with many Christians, believe that this valley and the Mount of Olives will be the scene of the resurrection and the final judgment. (Zech. 14:4

ILLUSTRATOR PHOTO/KEN TOUCHTON

Modern Church of All Nations, so-called because several nations shared in its building, dominates the lower slope of Gethsemane.

ILLUSTRATOR PHOTO/KEN TOUCHTON

prophesies that the end of days will be marked with the Mount of Olives violently splitting in two prior to the day of the coming of the Lord.) The Jews have an ancient tradition that the messianic reign will commence here on the Mount of Olives. So, from before the time of Christ, these slopes were sacred burial places. Three monumental tombs predominate in the valley: the onion-shaped domed "Pillar of Absalom"; the pyramid-topped tomb of Zechariah; and the columned tomb of St. James. All three of these tombs are from the Herodian era; the identifications are merely legendary.

ILLUSTRATOR PHOTO/KEN TOUCHTON

Opposite: The walled-in road behind the church leads past the Russian Church of St. Mary Magdalene and Dominus Flevit to the Eleona and Imbomon. The Tomb of Mary is to the left out of the picture. *Above:* So-called Tombs of James (left) and Zechariah. *Left:* So-called Tomb of Absalom.

ILLUSTRATOR PHOTO/KEN TOUCHTON

In addition to the Zechariah reference, the Mount of Olives is mentioned one more time in the Old Testament. David, unable to stem the revolt of Absalom, was forced to abandon his capital city. He took the path over the Mount of Olives on his way to temporary exile, fleeing barefoot along its steep path (2 Sam. 15:30).

In the days of Jesus, the Mount of Olives obviously was a lush, fertile, heavily-forested mountain, in contrast to today's barren slopes covered with stone houses, church buildings, and cemeteries. The very name, "Olives," indicates that the hill was covered with vast groves. Two villages on the eastern slopes of the Mount of Olives also suggest the fertility of the mountain: Bethphage (meaning "house of figs"), and Bethany (meaning "house of dates"). Gethsemane, located on the western slopes, means "olive press" or "vat."

To the city dwellers from the squalid streets and the crowded alleyways of Jerusalem, the Mount of Olives in Jesus' day offered a welcome place of refreshing retreat and escape. Thus we find the Mount of Olives prominently mentioned in the New Testament, especially during the last week of Jesus' ministry.

In the little village of Bethany (on the eastern side) lived Mary, Martha, and Lazarus. Jesus abode there at night after he taught in the Temple during the day (Luke 21:37). So our Lord crossed over the Mount of Olives several times during the last days of his ministry. Near Bethany, and on the southeastern slope of the Mount, is Bethphage where the disciples went to find a colt for the Master (Mark 11). From that area Jesus began his triumphal entry into Jerusalem, across the crest of the mountain and down past Gethsemane, over the Kidron Valley and up into the city through Stephen's Gate. Here on the slopes of the mountain Jesus used the sign of the withering of the barren fig tree to teach a lesson of stewardship (Mark 11:12-14). Here on the same slopes he gave the great eschatological discourse of Matthew 24.

On the western slope of the Mount of Olives is the garden of Gethsemane. All four Gospels record our Lord's agony, betrayal, and arrest in this garden (Matt. 26:36-56; Mark 14:32-45; Luke 22:39-53; John 18:1-12). The garden probably was a privately-owned olive grove. No doubt Jesus and his disciples were friends of the owner. The olive grove became a place of retreat for Jesus, and the garden was located at the grove's olive "press" or olive oil "vat." The spot seems to have been a familiar and favorite retreat for the Master and his disciples.

The location of Gethsemane today is based on a very early and probably quite reliable tradition. First references to the location are by the church historians Eusebius and Jerome. The present site was selected by Queen Helena, mother of Constantine, in AD 326. In the garden area are eight very ancient, gnarled olive trees. Their twisted trunks seem to reflect our Master's agony as he prayed in the garden. Josephus, the Jewish historian, records that the Roman general Titus cut down all the trees on the Mount of Olives in his destruction of Jerusalem in AD 70, so the present trees probably have come up from the roots of those trees of Jesus' day. Here in this garden Jesus prayed, "Not my will, but thine, be done" (Luke 22:42). Here he was betrayed by the kiss of Judas. Here he was arrested and carried away for trial as Peter sought to defend him from the mob and hacked off the ear of a Temple guard.

Today the modern Church of All Nations stands next to the garden. It is built over a rock that from a very early tradition has been identified as the spot where Jesus knelt and prayed. The first church built on this site was constructed in the fourth century. Later destroyed by the Persians in AD 614, it was rebuilt by the Crusaders and destroyed again in the fourteenth century. The present edifice was completed in 1924 on the foundations of the fourth-century church. Mosaic pavements from that early church still can be seen preserved in the floor.

The Church of All Nations received its name because contributions from around the world funded its construction. One of the twelve domes (in the southwest corner) commemorates the contribution of the United States. The dome is decorated with the Crusader cross in the center, the American eagle and the seal of the United States on the sides.

Other nearby church buildings—the seven-onion-domed Russian Church of St. Mary Magdalene, and the Russian Orthodox monastery with its magnificent tower on the summit—have no gospel connection (see photo 32, p. 112).

Directly above the garden of Gethsemane on the crest of the Mount of Olives is the Chapel of the Ascension. This site commemorates the ascension of our Lord (Luke 24:50-52; Acts 1:9, 12). In AD 378 a Roman lady named Pomenia built an octagonal-shaped church on this highest summit over a rock where, according to an early tradition, Jesus stood to address his disciples and then ascend into heaven. Many believe

The onion-domed Russian Church, built in 1888, commemorates Mary Magdalene.

ILLUSTRATOR PHOTO/DAVID ROGERS

To be buried in Jerusalem has long been a dream of pious Jews. These ancient tombs are on Mount Scopus just north of the Mount of Olives.

they can see the imprint of his foot miraculously recorded in the rock. For more than fifteen centuries, devout pilgrims from around the world have come to this site to read the account of our Lord's ascension and hear again the promise that "this same Jesus . . . shall so come in like manner" (Acts 1:11).

The early church building on this site of the ascension was destroyed in the seventh century, restored again by the Crusaders, taken over by the Moslems in the thirteenth century, and partially restored today. The small octagonal building covering the rock of the ascension remains Moslem property today.

The Mount of Olives is an authentic site. On its crest and around its slopes significant events in the life of our Lord took place. The fact that we are dependent on tradition rather than hard archeological evidence to confirm the exact location of these events does not diminish the authenticity of the happenings that took place here on the Mount of Olives. Whether from the stone in the Chapel of the Ascension or from some other stone very nearby, our Lord *did* ascend into heaven. Under olive trees in Gethsemane, these or others nearby, our Lord *did* kneel and pray. His feet *did* tread the ancient paths that still cross the brow of this hill connecting Bethany and Bethphage with Jerusalem. To visit the Mount of Olives today assuredly is to walk in the footsteps of the Master!

The Judgment Hall

W. Murray Severance

An amateur could examine the extensive remains of the Colosseum in Rome and, from the remaining structure, could closely reconstruct the appearance. The judgment hall in Jerusalem is a different story. Very little data remains—even in biblical accounts, Josephus, or later historians and archeologists. Only since the birth of modern biblical archeology has any scientific investigation taken place.

Two basic problems exist in regard to the location and description of the judgment hall; one is historical, the other archeological. The Bible states only that Pilate entered the Praetorium and asked Jesus if he were king of the Jews. Later, without explanation as to location, Pilate had Jesus "brought out" to the judgment seat at a place called the Pavement, and, in Hebrew, *Gabbatha*. There, with the persuasion of the chief priests, Pilate turned Jesus over to them to be led away to be crucified (John 18:33; 19:13-16).

Jerusalem is not a true *tell* (artificial hill); the present streets are up to thirty feet above the level of Jesus' day! Since Jerusalem still is an occupied city, access to property where archeologists can dig is very difficult to gain. In recent years, however, extensive digging has been possible in a number of areas in and around the Old City. Scant remains of the Tower of Antonia have been identified at the northwestern corner of the Temple platform. According to many archeologists, Antonia, the Praetorium, the Pavement (called the *Lithostrotos*), and the Judgment Hall are considered to be part of the same location. Antonia was the palace guard tower rebuilt by Herod the Great at the northwest corner of the Temple court and named in honor of Mark Antony. The Praetorium was all or part of the governor's official residence in Jerusalem. The Pavement was the courtyard of Pilate's headquarters at Antonia. Judgment hall is the King James Version translation of *praitorion* (praetorium).

The problem of identification of the judgment hall is historical. In AD 1109 Gesta Francorum wrote, "As to the scourging of Jesus, the crowning with thorns, the derision and other tortures that he endured for us, it is not easy to discern today where they happened since the city has been subsequently so often sacked and destroyed."[1] Other scholars and scientists in 1172, 1310, and later in 1873, 1910, and 1933 came to the same conclusions about the degree of difficulty. Based on findings, however, various religious orders and groups have committed themselves to sites and have built convents, monasteries, churches, chapels, sepulchers, schools, and hospices around and over these sacred sites. The pomp and circumstance of the trappings almost obliterate the significance of the original event.

The Tower of Antonia is not named specifically in the Bible, but is referred to as a barracks or castle. The citadel was built on the site of an earlier Maccabean stronghold. This Maccabean structure had been preceded by a fortress which Nehemiah erected when he rebuilt Jerusalem. Perhaps even Solomon had built a fortress on this site. Why? The location was ideally suited for defense even before a fortress was built. The terrain was precipitous on three sides. On the west the castle wall was built on the cliff edge of the Tyropean Valley, which is completely filled in today. The north wall was separated from the hill *Bezetha* by a wall and a deep moat. The south wall was on an escarpment seventy-five feet above the Temple area. The eastern area still is a matter of conjecture.

For better defense the rocky prominence was faced with smooth, slippery flagstones. Above the rock, stone walls rose another sixty feet. The citadel was roughly rectangular in shape (490' by 260') with four towers, one at each corner. The southeast tower was one hundred feet high, the others seventy-five feet (opinions vary on this point).

The structure served as a palace and as a barracks. The central court was reached by multiple staircases, which also led to apartments, cloisters, booths, baths, and barracks. Many scholars feel this is the court where a procurator might have delivered legal decisions as Pilate did concerning Jesus (John 19:13). Exact determination is difficult because Titus, between AD 66 and 70, completely destroyed Antonia. All that remains today on the site is some Herodian masonry in the lower courses of the modern barracks.

Above: Pilate Stone, found at Caesarea. *Right:* From model, the Antonia Fortress (note high towers to see into Temple area to right).

ILLUSTRATOR PHOTO/KEN TOUCHTON

LIBRARY OF CONGRESS/MATSON COLLECTION

This stone, located in the probable area of the Judgment Hall, has a game incised into it. Dating from the 2nd-3rd century AD, it helped Roman soldiers while away their time.

Recently, in 1972, a French scholar named P. Benoit investigated the stone pavement (*Lithostrotos*). His report came out under the auspices of the Israel Exploration Society in Jerusalem and was based in part on 1966 excavations in the Antonia area. Concerning the pavement, Benoit indicates that the courtyard stonework of Antonia generally is regarded as being from the time of Herod and was the place where Jesus was condemned. His conclusion that the paving blocks were placed there in the days of Hadrian (AD 117-138) is based on two other factors: the date of the famous triumphal arch "Ecce Homo" ("Behold the man") above the pavement and the vaulted pool called Struthion beneath the pavement.

According to Josephus (*Wars* V. iii. 2), the pool was still an open reservoir during the siege of Jerusalem in AD 70, for Titus built a ramp over it to gain access for his battering rams to the wall of Antonia. If so, then Antonia did not include this pool, which now is under a vaulted roof. Concerning the arch, the archeologists' investigation of 1966 concluded that it was built when the pavement was laid.[2] Since the arch was built during the time of Hadrian, so was the Pavement. The Pavement, now within the Convent of the Sisters of Zion, now is proved to be that of a small Roman forum built about one hundred years after Jesus was condemned. The shape of the most famous model of the Antonia fortress in the garden of the Holyland Hotel in Jerusalem also is now under severe questioning as to description.

We already have alluded to the question of location of the Judgment Hall. No viewpoint yet has been corroborated, but from available historical and archeological data the facts point to Herod's palace on the Western side of Jerusalem as the place of judgment. Josephus and Philo both testify that Roman governors stayed there while in Jerusalem. The Gospels' description suits this site better than any other, especially in light of the dating of the *Lithostrotos* as Hadrianic, not Herodian.

---

[1] Christopher Hollis and Ronald Brownrigg, *Holy Places* (London: Weidenfield & Nicolson, 1969), p. 156.
[2] Kathleen Kenyon, *Digging Up Jerusalem* (New York: Praeger Publishers, 1974), pp. 260-261.

Where Is Golgotha?

Joseph A. Callaway

The vertically-dressed ledge of pinkish-gray stone spread in front of the seated tourists like a curtain across a stage. A rectangular doorway in the center broke the rather blank expanse of the Garden Tomb (see photo 31, p. 112) and opened into its rock-cut chamber. I stood at the back of the group and listened as the wondrous passage of John's Gospel about Mary finding the empty tomb was read once again.

The implication was clear. Here at the feet of these silent worshipers was one thing they came to Jerusalem to see and touch: the actual tomb where our Lord lay and where Mary made that emotional discovery about twenty centuries ago. A stone's throw away on the right is the rocky knoll pointed out as Golgotha, now a Moslem cemetery.

My thoughts were racing across the centuries in search of Mary's experience when a student who stood beside me broke the spell of the moment with a blunt question. "Is this really the Garden Tomb," he wanted to know, "and is that hill Golgotha?"

The inflection of his voice told me he wanted a straight answer. He couldn't reach out to identify with Mary's sorrow until the facts were right in his mind.

"Does it matter whether this is actually the place?" I asked.

"Yes," he responded. "I have read that Gordon's selection of this place as Golgotha was based on very little factual evidence, and I can't

The Garden Tomb cannot be authentic, but its atmosphere is much more worshipful than that of the cluttered Church of the Holy Sepulchre.

ILLUSTRATOR PHOTO/DAVID ROGERS

Below: Gordon's Calvary, only recently claimed as authentic, has Moslem graveyard on its summit. *Opposite:* Covering for the traditional hole in which the cross was set, Church of the Holy Sepulchre.

ILLUSTRATOR PHOTO/DAVID ROGERS

ignore the feeling that it is false to treat it as the authentic one."

"All right," I replied. "Let's go over to the observation platform in front of Gordon's Calvary and talk awhile."

We followed a winding path to a concrete platform in front of the cliff, and I invited the student to sit with me on a bench at the edge of the platform. The cliff, with its cavern-like holes that suggest eye sockets and nose bridge of a skull, loomed over us.

"At the outset," I began, "you should recognize two things. First, there have been too many destructions and rebuildings of Jerusalem since the first century for us to recover much of the city of that time. I doubt, for instance, that we could ever say with finality that a certain place is Golgotha or that a certain tomb is the one in which Jesus was buried. And second, the unquestioned authenticity of specific places is not nearly as important to most people who come here as it is to you."

"What do you mean?" the student interrupted.

"Well, take this week for instance. There are probably two thousand Christian tourists in Israel, and they are busy visiting two Gethsemanes, two Golgothas, and two tombs of Joseph of Arimathea. Now, if they were overly concerned with authenticity, how could they live with *two* holy places where individual events occurred?"

"I hadn't thought of it in that way," he mused.

"Most people who come here want a convenient place sanctioned by people of their faith where they can relive events in a spiritual experience. They come to worship, not to inquire, and the memory of an experience is what they take home. Many of them never get dates and places and names sorted out, and they certainly don't get involved in the factual evidence of conflicting places."

"Maybe you are right," the student conceded. "But two Golgothas bother me, and I would like to know something about each one. What does this place we're looking at now, Gordon's Calvary, have going for it?"

I pondered his question a moment because I knew we were setting off on an issue laden with emotion.

"The rocky hill we see here," I began, "first was proposed as Golgotha in 1842 by Otto Thenius, a German. He was drawn to the site by the appearance of the cliff and its proximity to the Damascus Gate. The Garden Tomb that we saw a moment ago was found a quarter of a century later, in 1867, and had no influence on Thenius. In fact, very few people gave a second thought to the site before General Charles 'Chinese' Gordon came to Jerusalem in 1883-84 and asserted in an article in 1885 that this was, indeed, the location of Golgotha and the Garden Tomb."

"And there are no ancient traditions locating Golgotha at this place?" the student asked.

"Not that I know of," I answered. "General Gordon seems to have begun the modern tradition. His reasons, which are not widely known, fit very well into the pattern of tradition-making."

"Yes?"

"Yes," I replied. "He saw the holes in the cliff that he called Skull Hill. The clincher for his identification was an interpretation of Leviticus 1:11 that says the sacrificial victims are to be slain on the altar northwards, 'literally, to be slain slantwise or askew on the north of the altar.'[1] He drew a line north from the Temple altar, then drew another north-northwest, or 'askew' toward Skull Hill, and reasoned that Christ, as the 'Prototype' sacrifice, would be slain there on Skull Hill, askew or slantwise from the north of the altar.[2] Thus he 'proved' his site, the one we are looking at now, to be the true Golgotha, mentioned in Matthew 27:33 and Mark 15:22 as 'the place of a skull.'"

"But that is a rather farfetched idea!" the student exclaimed. "Is there any support from archeology of the location?"

Above: Roman nails, 1*st* century AD. *Top:* The cutaway stone of Calvary, viewed through narrow slot, is protected by marble; Church of the Holy Sepulchre.

"Very little, if any," I said. "There would be nothing but rocks left on Golgotha, so the archeologist has to work with the tomb."

"Does anything remain from the Garden Tomb?" he asked.

"Not much, because it was discovered in 1867, the year of the first excavations in Palestine in modern times. There is, however, a record of bones being found in the tomb, and two red Byzantine crosses were painted on the east wall inside, opposite the rectangular doorway."

"Does this mean that the Garden Tomb is Byzantine, dating to the fith or sixth centuries AD?"

"Probably," I answered. "People in the Byzantine period either reused older tombs or hewed out new ones. This one shows no evidence of earlier use, dating back to the time of Christ. In fact, its form is that of a fifth-century tomb."

"How do you know?" he queried.

"Byzantine tombs have trough-like places in the burial chamber where bodies were placed, just like the two places in the Garden Tomb, and they did not have rolling stone doors. First-century Jewish tombs, on the other hand, used either long lateral shafts cut into the walls of the burial chamber for individual burials, or elevated shelves under low arches, also cut into the stone sides of the chamber. These tombs were closed by large rolling stones shaped like thick stone wheels. The Garden Tomb has neither the first-century niches for burial nor a rolling stone door closure."

"But isn't there a place for a rolling stone door at the Garden Tomb?" the student persisted.

"I don't believe the wide groove below the doorway was cut for a rolling stone," I replied. "Rolling stone doors are not made that way. You can see an authentic one at the Herodian family tomb hear the King David Hotel, west of the Jaffa Gate. I think the Garden Tomb had a Byzantine-type hinged rectangular stone door that opened inward into the first chamber."

"A hinged stone door?"

"Yes, hinged and swinging just like the front

Left: Earthquake crack below where the cross was placed (close-up below). *Bottom right:* Slab marking traditional spot where Jesus' body laid when removed from cross. *Bottom left:* Close-up of slab.

173

door of your house. I helped excavate one on Mount Ebal near Nablus in 1964 that was in original condition, even to iron hinges and latches that still worked. The door fit into a carved recess on the inside of the opening, just like the recess inside the opening of the Garden Tomb. And I noticed a piece of iron hardware that was still in the inner face of this opening."

"So you think the Garden Tomb is Byzantine and not the tomb of Jesus?" he asked.

"Right," I answered. "And that leads me to reject Gordon's Calvary as Golgotha also."

"Couldn't there be first-century tombs here that would change your mind about Golgotha?" he continued.

"There could be, but they have not been found," I said. "Until they are found, I'll have to prefer the Church of the Holy Sepulcher location of Golgotha and the tomb because the archeological evidence and tradition favor it."

"Are there tombs there like those you described?"

"Yes," I answered. "You can see a first-century tomb with lateral burial shafts right behind the Coptic part of the Holy Sepulcher; and a first-century shell tomb was found under the Coptic monastery in 1885 when a cistern was being dug at the edge of the church. These are

ILLUSTRATOR PHOTO/KEN TOUCHTON

ILLUSTRATOR PHOTO/DAVID ROGERS

tombs from the time of Jesus; indeed, Jesus seems to have been buried in a shelf-type tomb like the one under the Coptic monastery."

"The Church of the Holy Sepulcher has more than just tradition going for it then," the student said.

"It has tradition *and* archeological evidence, even though we are still turned off by the shrine-like trappings of statues, candles, gifts, and chanting priests. And, you know, one other thing about the Garden Tomb and Gordon's Calvary strikes me as ironic."

"Ironic?"

"Yes, ironic," I replied. "The Garden Tomb seems to be part of a cemetery associated with St. Stephen's Church across the north wall of the garden property. This church was built right after the Church of the Holy Sepulchre, early in the fifth century. In one tomb near St. Stephen's Church, and contemporary with the Garden Tomb, was an inscription reading. 'Tomb of the deacon Nonnus Onesimus of the Holy Anastasis of Christ and of this monastery.'"

"What's ironic about that?" the student asked, puzzled.

"The Church of the Holy Sepulcher was first called the 'Holy Anastasis,' after the Greek word *anastasis* for 'resurrection,'" I said. "And Onesimus, who was buried in a tomb contemporary with and near the Garden Tomb, was a deacon in that church. The irony is that the Garden Tomb may have been the burial place of a deacon of the original Church of the Holy Sepulchre and some of us are regarding his burial place as that of the Lord himself."

"Well, if you think Golgotha and the tomb of Jesus are at the Church of the Holy Sepulcher," he asked, "why were you so wrapped up in the worship service back there at the Garden Tomb?"

"That's a fair question I hadn't put to myself," I responded. "Let's say it's easier for me to recapture the wonder of the resurrection in front of the simple tomb of a Byzantine Christian than it is amid the gloomy distraction of the more authentic site."

Opposite, top: Marble-covered spot inside tomb where Jesus' body was laid, Church of the Holy Sepulchre. *Opposite, bottom:* Rolling-stone entrance to Herod's family tomb. *Above:* Entrance to Church of the Holy Sepulchre.

---
[1] Charles Gordon, "Golgotha," *Palestine Exploration Fund Quarterly Statement,* 1885, p. 79.
[2] *Ibid.*

Emmaus

Joe O. Lewis

The account of Jesus' appearance to Cleopas and another disciple on the road to Emmaus is a favorite with people whose hearts likewise have burned within them after their encounters with Jesus. It has been a favorite of New Testament scholars in recent years, too, as a long list of learned articles can testify. The only people who have problems with this beautiful and moving account are the geographers and archeologists. They haven't been able to find Emmaus! Indeed, the problems associated with locating Emmaus appear to be virtually unsolvable. Perhaps it's just as well, for Luke certainly never intended to give his readers a lesson in geography when he recorded this meeting. Now that you've been forewarned that this chapter will leave you wondering about Emmaus, let's look at the problems and solutions surrounding the site.

Luke mentioned a village named Emmaus toward which Cleopas and another disciple walked on the day the empty tomb was discovered (Luke 24:13). At some point on that journey Jesus joined them, but they did not recognize him until they reached the village and ate with him that evening. These two disciples then hurried back to Jerusalem to tell "the eleven" and the others what had happened to them.

According to the Greek text, the distance from Jerusalem to Emmaus was 60 stadia (the King James Version has threescore furlongs; the Revised Standard Version and most other recent

'Amwas, one of the claimants to be Emmaus, now is a park area.

ILLUSTRATOR PHOTO/KEN TOUCHTON

translations have 7 miles). However, one important manuscript and several of lesser importance record the distance as 160 stadia, which is 20 miles. A stadium (stadia is the plural) normally measured 195 meters, or 607 feet. A furlong now is set at one-eighth of a mile, or 220 yards. Thus, the first problem we face in locating Emmaus is to decide which manuscript to go by. Emmaus was either some seven miles or some twenty miles from Jerusalem. As you can tell, most modern translations assume the shorter distance. Why?

Two major considerations govern this decision. The primary one is the time factor involved in making a return trip to Jerusalem from Emmaus after the evening meal. If the distance were 20 miles (160 stadia), the return trip on foot would have taken at least 5 hours at a brisk pace and probably longer; the return trip would have been up hill. Since Luke did not mention any change in the mode of transportation, there is no reason to assume that the two disciples used horses or donkeys for the return.

Another major reason for rejecting the longer distance is the scholarly deduction that the reading that is most difficult to explain is likely to be the original one. As you will learn below, there was a well-known Emmaus located about twenty miles from Jerusalem. Scholars assume that a well-known site might have caused a later scribe to add one hundred stadia to the original sixty in order to make the text fit his facts. It is difficult to see why a scribe would have deleted one hundred stadia to make the text refer to a site that was unknown.

Several possible locations have been suggested for Emmaus. The oldest and best-known location is an Emmaus located twenty miles from Jerusalem. Today this ancient city is simply a village lying around the corner from better-known places. It is called 'Amwas. On April 27,

ILLUSTRATOR PHOTO/KEN TOUCHTON

Left: A modern road runs from 'Amwas park to Jerusalem. *Right:* The village has been removed and trees planted on the tell.

Sites that claim to be Emmaus

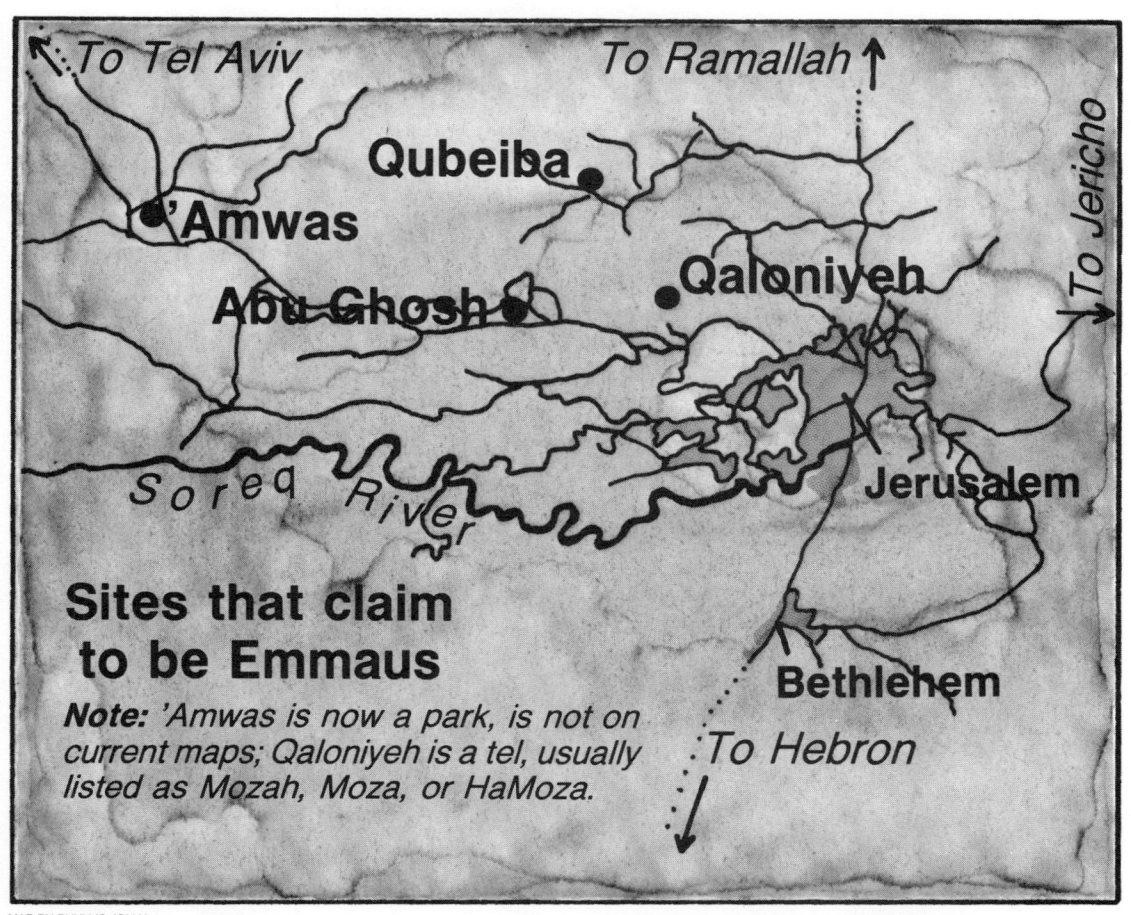

Note: 'Amwas is now a park, is not on current maps; Qaloniyeh is a tel, usually listed as Mozah, Moza, or HaMoza.

MAP BY PHYLLIS JOLLY

ILLUSTRATOR PHOTO/KEN TOUCHTON

1852, Edward Robinson and a company of travelers described how they came to the site:

> 'Amwas, lying on the gradual western declivity of a rocky hill, sufficiently high to have an extensive view of the great plain. It is now a poor hamlet consisting of a few mean houses. There are two fountains or wells of living water; one just by the village, and the other a little down the shallow valley west.[1]

ILLUSTRATOR PHOTO/KEN TOUCHTON

Although this Emmaus is not referred to in the Old Testament, it is mentioned in the Apocrypha. A famous battle took place there between Judas Maccabaeus and the Syrian general Gorgias in the second century BC (1 Maccabees 3; 4). Later the Syrians refortified the site. Under the Romans the city grew in importance until its fortunes changed and it was reduced first to slavery and then burned. The burning took place just after Herod the Great died. Two hundred years later the city received a new name, Nicopolis, by which it was known for centuries.

When Robinson arrived in 1852, the remains of an old church still were visible. Excavations have shown that the church dates to the rebuilding of Emmaus-Nicopolis in the third century AD; however, nothing in the church served to link it to the biblical episode related by Luke. Robinson thought that 'Amwas, without doubt, was the Emmaus Luke intended. It is true, as he noted, that from the time of the earliest Christian writers up to the fourteenth century AD no other opinion ever was advanced. He assumed that scribes not familiar with the geography of Palestine (that is, those living in Rome, Antioch, or Alexandria) accidentally left out the word for "one hundred" as they copied the Greek text, thus causing today's problem. He also argued that if the travelers had left 'Amwas at six o'clock in the evening they could have reached Jerusalem by eleven o'clock that night, in time to meet the assembled disciples of Jesus.

Other scholars are not convinced of the accuracy of Robinson's reasoning. All modern versions of the Bible accept the reading "60 stadia" rather than "160 stadia" as the more accurate one. Thus, these scholars prefer to look elsewhere for the biblical Emmaus. In the fourteenth century AD, for reasons unknown to anyone, Emmaus began to be identified with a place called *Kubeibeh*. The identification of Kubeibeh with Emmaus may be linked to a group of Crusaders of the eleventh century AD who claimed that Kubeibeh residents called their vil-

The cruciform baptistry (opposite) and basilica ruins (above) at 'Amwas date in earlier phases to the 3rd century, an early date for a commemorative church building.

lage Emmaus. Kubeibeh is the correct distance from Jerusalem, about seven miles northwest of the city. In the mid-nineteenth century a group of Catholics purchased a site at Kubeibeh and sought to fix this location as Emmaus. Since then excavations have been conducted on the site, and remains of a church dating back at least to Crusader times have been discovered.

Another site that has been identified with Emmaus is *Qaloniyeh,* called Mozah in the Old Testament (Josh. 18:26). The Jewish historian Josephus mentioned an Emmaus at this place where Vespasian settled eight hundred veterans. Josephus specifically located this Emmaus thirty stadia from Jerusalem (*Wars of the Jews;* VII; 6; 6). However, the Arab village of Qaloniyeh is only four miles west of Jerusalem on the road to Jaffa; thus doubt is cast on the location referred to by Josephus.

Still another place that some have identified with Emmaus is *Abu Ghosh,* ancient *Kiriath Jearim* of the Old Testament. It is about nine miles from Jerusalem and between Qaloniyeh and 'Amwas. The Romans made this village a military outpost to guard the Jerusalem road. Part of the Tenth Legion was stationed there. No ancient evidence fixes the site of Emmaus there, however.

'Amwas and Kubeibeh remain as the two most probable locations of Emmaus. The former has the more ancient tradition, but the latter fits the geography of Luke 24:13-35 better. Fortunately for Christians, the message of joyous surprise that shines through the passage does not depend on the location of the events. It is enough to know that the disciples were returning to their homes when Jesus appeared to them as a traveling companion.

---
[1] Edward Robinson et al., *Biblical Researches in Palestine and the Adjacent Regions.* 3(1856), 146.

ILLUSTRATOR PHOTO/KEN TOUCHTON

Where Did the Ascension Take Place?

W. Murray Severance

The Greek words, "as far as Bethany," in Luke 24:50 (RSV) may be translated in several ways: "to the neighborhood of Bethany," "over against Bethany," or "out to the vicinity of Bethany." The phrase plays an important role in locating the last appearance and ascension of Jesus.

The traditional view holds the site to be on Mount Olivet between Jerusalem and Bethany. Jesus and the disciples came from Jerusalem and were "in the vicinity of" Bethany. After the ascension, Acts 1:12 states: "they [the disciples] returned to Jerusalem from the mount called Olivet, which is near Jerusalem, [not farther than] a sabbath day's journey away" (RSV). The sabbath day's journey was a maximum distance the rabbinic law allowed Jews to walk on the sabbath, as described below. The location of the Mount of Olives meets the requirements of the law.

Numbers 35:5, according to some scholars, is the basis of the interpretation for the sabbath day's journey, first mentioned in Exodus 16:29. The Numbers passage defines the suburbs, or extent of a city, as being two thousand cubits in all directions from the city walls. On the sabbath, a faithful Jew would not travel farther than this. Other scholars use as a basis Joshua 3:4,

Mount of Olives (center) seen from south of the Temple Mount.

The Chapel of the Ascension, Crusader-built but now a mosque, is on a site called the Inbomon commemorated at least since the fourth century.

RELIGIOUS NEWS SERVICE

where God told the Israelites to separate themselves from the ark of the covenant two thousand cubits.

Josephus refers to the sabbath day's journey as five to six furlongs, or between 3,031 and 3,637 feet, as measured by the Alexandrine stadion or furlong. The cubit is not quite so definitive, but by the Hellenistic (Greek) measurement, 2,000 cubits would work out to be about 3,000 feet, or about 3,600 by the Roman measurement. From the eastern gate of Jerusalem, across the Kidron Valley, and up by Gethsemane to the crest of the hill called Olive's Orchard, the distance is about two-thirds of a mile, falling well within the limits of any of these reckonings. Bethany would be too far, but Luke does not state that Jesus led the disciples all the way to Bethany.

What historical structures exist today to mark the site of the ascension? The present-day tourist is taken to a rather forlorn-looking chapel up behind Gethsemane near the crest of the hill. Even the laymen can spot a mixture of architecture in the small octagon-shaped building. What once were openings now are walled up with stone. A conical roof was added by the Moslems in AD 1187. Some years earlier the Crusaders erected the unadorned building with an open ceiling on the site of the traditional spot from which Christ ascended. It is now controlled by the Moslems, who also believe in the ascension of Jesus.

All Christians are allowed to venerate the site. Inside, the tourist is shown a legendary footprint left by the ascending Christ. This is the *Inbomon,* a rendering in Latin of the Greek phrase *en bohmoh,* which means "upon this height."

The nun Aetheria reported that at least by about AD 385 the ascension was localized at a place on the very summit of the Mount of Olives. On Palm Sundays, even today, the Armenians, Coptics, and Syrians celebrate on the ninth hour at their respective altars inside the stone walls of the courtyard that surrounds the shrine.

Dominus Flevit (upper right) commemorates where Jesus wept over Jerusalem (Luke 19:41); the traditional place of the Ascension is just up the hill from this chapel.

Several other buildings connected with Jesus' last days and ascension are in the immediate vicinity. The most visible one is a tall, slim, soaring church bell tower called the Russian Candle of the Holy Land. It marks the Orthodox location of the ascension. It is six stories high and is tall enough that from it a tourist can see all the way down to Jericho and the Jordan River. At the southeast corner of the church building is a stone reputedly marking the place where Mary, the mother of Jesus, stood at the time of the ascension (see photo 44, p. 111).

Scanty remains of a church lie nearby. It is the *Eleona,* from a Greek word interpreted as *Olivet.* Excavations indicate that the earlier buildings on this site are even older than the *Inbomon* site. Ancient writers rank *Eleona* the third of the holy grottoes, together with that of Bethlehem (birth) and the holy spulcher (resurrection). Reputedly, this is the place where Jesus taught his disciples about the end of his physical presence on earth.

Most of the original shrines in and around Jerusalem were begun during the Byzantine period. This was a time when it became important to commemorate events, especially from the life of Christ. The greatest eastern landmark in Jerusalem then was a gleaming cross by day and a glowing lantern at night from the Church of the Ascension. Only the small octagonal Moslem mosque already described marks the spot today. In AD 378, a wealthy Roman lady named Pomonia, provided the funds for this first Ascension sanctuary. Until 1979, when the Franciscan fathers carried out extensive excavations on the Mount of Olives, the only report of this original building had come from a traveling Gallic bishop in AD 670.

As time turns back, we come finally to the accounts of the Gospel writers. Note carefully a decided change from the pens of these biblical historians and following secular reporters. The Gospel writers had no buildings to describe, nor any legendary footprints to account for. They majored on the happening, not on a site. Only two scant accounts, one in Luke 24:50 and one in Acts 1:12 give us clues as to where Jesus ascended. "And Jesus led them out to the vicinity of Bethany . . ." and when he had ascended, "they returned unto Jerusalem from the mount called Olivet, which is from Jerusalem a sabbath day's journey."

Index

'Abarah: 43
Abdullah Bridge: 43
Abila: 91,94
Abu Ghosh: 181
Aelia Capitolina: see "Jerusalem"
Aenon: 40
Aetheria: 57,59,62,131,185
Afula: 30
ain et-Tabighah: 64
Akra: 100
Alexander the Great: 22-23,53,86,91,92,99
Allenby Bridge: 43
Amathus: 94
Amman: 44,93
'Amwas: 178,180,181; *photos* 176-181
Anonymous of Piacenza: 57,62
Antiochia: see "Hippos"
Antioch on the Chrysorhoas: see "Gerasa"
Antipator: 26,100
Antonia Fortress: 100,101,102,104,117,120,144; *photo* 164-165; see also "Judgment Hall"
Apocrypha: 180; see also individual books
Arabia: 46
Araq el-Emir: 94
Arbela: 75
Arculf: 41,156
Ariston: 92
Ark of the Covenant: *photo* 59
Artemis, temple of: 92
Ascension: 183-186
Assyria: 22
Augustus: 27,63,89,90,101,104; *photos* 13,32
Babylon: 22
Banias: 39,86; *photo* 87
Baptism: 38,39-43; *photos* 41,113,180
Bartimaeus: 140
Beautiful Gate: 149,152; *photo* 152
Beni Hazir tomb: 100
Bethabara: 41-43
Bethany: near Jerusalem: 41,46,131,160,183,185; *photo* 70,134 beyond Jordan: 41-43

Beth-aramphtha: 94
Bethel: 33,54; *photo* 33
Bethesda Pool: 100,117,118-121; *photos* 118-119
Bethlehem: 13-18; *photos* 12-19,65
Bethphage: 160
Bethsaida-Julius: 63-64,74,77
Beth-shean: 39,40,57,86,88,91; *photos* 40,72,88,89
Beth-yerah: 75,77
Bezetha (Bethesda): 102,164
Bira: 33; *photo* 35
Birah: 100
Birket Mousa: 138
Bordeaux Pilgrim: 50
Caesarea Maritima: 41
Caesarea Philippi: 86-87; *photos,* 86,87
Caiaphas' House: 116; *photo* 95
Callirhoe: 94
Cana: 49
Canatha: 87
Capernaum: 57-62,74,75; *photos* 56-62
Cardo: 113
Caves:
  Room of St. Joseph, 17
  Crypt of the Innocent Children, 17
  Shepherd's Field, 18
Carmel, 20
Cenacle: see "Upper Room"
Chinnereth, Lake of: see "Sea of Galilee"
Chinnereth, town: 73-74
"Christ Tempted": 48-49
Churches:
  Annunciation, Nazareth: 24; *photo* 21
  Emmaus, 'Imwas: *photos* 180,181
  Gerasa: 92; *photos* 92,93
  Jacob's Well: 51
  Marionite, Leap of the Precipice: 25
  Melchite, Bethlehem: 25
  Mount Gerizim:55
  Nativity, Bethlehem: 13-17; *photos* 14-19,66,67
  Peter's House, Capernaum: 62
  St. Joseph, Nazareth: 24-25
Churches, Jerusalem:
  Agony: 116
  All Nations: 160-161; *photos* 157,158

Ascension: 115,161,186; *photo* 184-185
Dominus Flevit: *photo* 111
Dormition: 156; *photo* 156
Eleona: 186
Hagia Zion: 116,156; *photos* 171-175
Holy Sepulchre: 102,115,117,156,174-175
Inbomon: 185
Nea: 116, *photo* 117
St. Anne: 117,119,121; *photos* 118,119
St. Mary Magdalene, Russian: 161,186; *photos* 111,161
St. Peter of Gallicantu: *photo* 111
St. Stephen: 116,175
Citadel: 100,101,102,116; *photos* 97,105
Claudius, Emperor: 28
Cleopatra: 136
Coenaculum: 116
Constantine: 14,17,25,113,115, 160; *photo* 14
Crusaders: 17,46,51,75,113,160, 162,181,185
Cyrus Cylinder: *photo* 71
Damascus Gate: 102,116,117,171; *photo* 98
David's Tower: 116; *photo* 97
Dead Sea Scrolls: see "Qumran"
Decapolis: 86-93
Deir er-Ra'ouat: 18
Dion: 89
Dome of the Rock: 131,153; *photos* 107,153
Dothan: 31; *photo* 31
Double Gate: 116,147; *photos* 99,112,148
Dung Gate: 104
Ebal, Mount: 50,53,174
Ecce Homo: 167
Ecclesiasticus: 136
Ein Gev: 77,83
Ain Karim: *photo* 36
el-Azariyeh: 131
Eleona: 115
el-Eizariyeh: 131
el Hajlah: 43
Emmaus: 176-181; *photos* 176-181
Endor: 30
en-Rogel: 96,116
Esbus: 94

187

Esdraelon plain: see "Jezreel"
es-Sakhra: 153
Essenes: 36,104; see also "Qumran"
et-Tell: 63
Eudocia, Queen: 116; *photo* 116
Eusebius: 40,92,115,136,160
Fahil: 91
Feasts:
   Passover: 55,83,132,140,155, 142,152
   Pentecost: 55,155
   Tabernacles: 55,137,151
   Day of Atonement: 100,151
Felix, procurator: 29
Fishing: *photos* 74-76
Gabbatha: see "Judgment Hall"
Gabinius: 136
Gadara: 90
Gadarene: 77,83,90
Galilee: 22,23,26,40,63-64, 84,135
Garden Tomb: 168,171,172,174,175; *photos* 112,168-169
Gennesar: 74
Gennesaret Plain: 74,84
Gerasa: 92,93,94; *photos* 71,90-93
Gerizim, Mount: 32,50,53-55; *photos* 52,54,55.
Gethsemane: 131,157-162,185; *photos* 157-162
Gibeon: 33; *photo* 34
Gihon Spring: 96,97,101,116, 122-129; *photos* 122-125,127
Gilboa, Mount: 31,82
Gilead: 40,92-94; *photo* 72
Golan Heights: 77,93
Golden Gate: 149; *photo* 109
Golgotha: 168-175; *photos* 170,171-174
Gordon's Calvary: 171,174,175
Great Confession: 86
Grotto: see "Cave"
Hadrian, Emperor: 13,55,104,115,155,156,167
Hammath: 90
Haram esh-Sherif: see "Temple Mount"
Hasmoneans: see "Maccabees"
Helena: 14,160
Hermon, Mount: 83,86
Herod:
   Agrippa I: 28,60,102,104, 120; *photo* 98
   Agrippa II: 29,104
   Antipas: 23,27,38,74,75,94
   Antipater: 139
   Archelaus: 101,139
   the Great: 18,27,46-47, 63,86,89,90,93,94,99, 100,101,120,137,138,139, 163,180; see also "Temple"
   Herodias: 38
   Salome: 139
   Tomb: *photo* 174
Herodium: 18,138,139; *photos* 18,19,65
Herod's palace: 100,102,167; *photo* 105
Hezekiah's Pool: 101
Hezekiah's Tunnel: 95
Hezekiah's Wall: *photo* 106
Hinnom: 96,102,104; *photos* 96,105
Hippicus tower: 100
Hippos: 77,89
Horns of Hattin: 75,79
Huldah Gates: see "Double Gate," "Triple Gate"
Huleh, Lake: 84
Inn of the Good Samaritan: 141
Irbid: 91
Israel Pool: 101,117,144
Jebusite wall: *photo* 106
Jacob's Well: 32,157; *photo* 50
Jaffa Gate: 116,117,172
Jenin: 31
Jerash: see "Gerasa"
Jericho: 39,44,45,46, 135-141,186; *photos* 108,112,135, 140-141
Jerome: 17,136,160
Jerusalem: 35,54, 95-117,135,155-156; *photos* 95-119,122-129 (see also individual entries)
Jezreel: 22,30,39,88; *photo* 69
John the Baptist: 36-38, 39-43,49,63; *photos* 36-43
   Monastery of: 41
Jordan Valley: 37,38,39-43, 44-47,58,86,87,88,94,97,135, 138,186; *photos* 42,44-45,87,108
Joseph of Arimathea: 171
Joseph, St., Room of: 17
Joseph, St., Tomb of: 50; *photo* 53
Josephus, Flavius: 29,53,54,55,136,157,160, 163,181,185
Judas of Galilee: 27
Judgment Hall: 100,163-167; *photos* 164-167
Julian the Apostate, Emperor: 113
Justin: 13,14
Justinian, Emperor: 17,55,116
Kathros House: 104
Kefar Nahum: 58
Khirbet el-'Araj: 63,77
Kidron Valley: 18,46,96,100, 101,102,131, 142,147,157,160,185; *photo* 111
"Kingdom Come": 79-81
Kubeibeh: 180-181
Kursi: 77,90
Lachish letters: *photo* 105
Lazarium: see "Lazarus' Tomb"
Lazarus' Tomb: 131-134; *photos* 130-133
Lepers: 31
Lithostrotos: see "Judgment Hall"
Livias: 94
Lord's Supper: 155
Lower City, Jerusalem: 102; *photo* 150-151
Maccabees: 23,75,77,100,135,136, 137,139,163,180; *photos* 97,108
   Alexander Jannaeus: 23,26,77,89, 90,91,92,100
   Alexandra: 137
   Antigonus: 137
   Aristobulus: 23,100,137
   John Hyrcanus: 55
   Salome Alexandra: 100
   Simon the Hasmonean: 136,139
Machaerus: 38,94; *photo* 38
Madeba map: 40,156; *photos* 43,106
Magdala, Migdal: 57,74,75; *photo* 74-75
Makhtesh: 98
Manuscripts:
   Sahidic: 41
   Syriac: 41
Maps:
   Bethesda (Bezetha): 121
   Bethsaida: 63
   Central Nazareth: 24
   Emmaus sites: 179
   New Testament Jericho location: 137
   New Testament Jericho sites: 138
   Qumran: 38

Road from Nazareth to Jerusalem, the: 33
Siloam-Gihon: 126
Upper Room: 155
Wilderness of John's Baptizing, the: 40
Mariamne Tower: 100
Mark Antony: 94,136,163
Mar Saba: 18
Mary:
 annunciation: 24; *photo,* 22
 Well: 24
Masada: 46,138
Masonic Hall: see "Xystos"
Megiddo: 30,88; *photo* 68
Meleager: 90
Messiah: 36,38,48-49,79-81
Millo: 97
Millstone: *photo* 59
Mishneh: 98
Mizpeh: 35
Moab: 44,46
Moreh, Hill of: 82
Moriah: 153
Mount of Beatitudes: 74
Mount of Offense: 157
Mount of Olives:
 44,45,46,131,141,157-162, 183,185; *photos* 157-162, 182-183
Museum, Rockefeller (Palestine) Archaeological: 117
Synagogues:
 Capernaum: 58-59; *photos* 56,59,62
 Jerusalem: 104
 Nazareth: 25; *photo,* 23
 Tiberius: 75
Nabatea: 86,93,94
Nablus: 32,50,51,55,157,174; *photo* 30
Nain: 30,82; *photo* 82
Nazareth: 20-25,30; *photo* 25
Nazareth Decree: 20
Nebo, Mount: 45
Nicanor Gate: 101,149,151,152,153; *photo* 152
Nicopolis: 180
Ophel: 96,97,101,102,122
Origen: 13,41
Paneas: see "Banias"
Parthians: 27
Pavement: see "Judgment Hall"
Pella: 91-92,94
Perdiccas: 92
Perea: 86,94; *photo* 72
Persia: 14,22

Peter's House: 59-62; *photo* 61
Petra: 46,86
Phasael Tower: 100
Philadelphia: 93
Philip the Tetrarch: 63,64,86
Philo: 167
Philoteria: 77
Pilate: 18,55,101,164; *photo* 164
Pomenia: 161,186
Pompey: 26,89,90,91,100,136
Pool of the Towers: see "Hezekiah's Pool"
Praetorium: see "Judgment Hall"
Precipice, Leap of the: 25; *photo* 25
Ptolemies: 23,26,86,94,136
 III Euergetes: 91,99
 II Philadelphus: 77,93
Qaloniyeh: 181
Qanawat: 87
Quarantana: 46-47; *photo* 46-47
Qumran: 36,37; *photo* 11
Rachel's Tomb: 18; *photo* 18
Ramallah: 33,35; *photo* 35
Raphana: 87
Resurrection: 49
Revolt, Jewish: 27,29,55,60, 74-75,104,136
Robinson's Arch: 147; *photos* 146-147
Roman, Rome: 23,26, 27,29,46,55,63,75,79-81, 86,89,92,100,102,104,138, 155,181; *photos* 8,74,75,135,172
Salim: 40
Salome: 38
Samaria, region: 31,37,54,157; *photo* 31
Samaria, city: 31-32,135
Samaritans: 14,22,26,32,50-51,53-55; *photo* 54-55
Samaritan Temple: 55
Sanhedrin: 29,147,151
Scopus, Mount: 101, 104,116,157
Scythian: 89
Scythopolis: see "Beth-shean"
Sea of Galilee: 39,43,57,58,63,73-77, 83-84,86,87,90,92; *photos* 58,64,71-77,85
Seleucia: see "Abila"
Seleucids: 23,86,91,93,94,99, 100
 Antiochus III: 90,91,93

Antiochus IV Epiphanes: 92,100
Sepphoris: 23,25,26-29,75; *photos,* 26-29
Sermon on the Mount: 74,75,78
Seven Springs: see "Tabgha"
Shechem: *photo* 52
Sheep Pool: 120
Shepherd's Field: 13,18; *photo* 19
Shiloh: 33; *photo* 33
Shuneum: 30
Sidon: 86
Siloam Pool: 95,98,101, 116,119,122-129; *photos* 128,129
Siloam Inscription: 126-127; *photo* 127
Silwan: 129
sirocco: 83
Siyar el-ghanam: 18
Shechem: 53
Solomon's Stables: 146
soreq: 149
Stephen's Gate: 160
Storms: 83-84
Strabo: 136
Struthion Cistern: 101,167
Susita: see "Hippos"
Sychar: 49,50
Tabaqat Fahl: 91
Tabgha: 57,61,74
Tabor, Mount: 30,82,86; *photo* 31
Taurus: 136
Teacher of Righteousness: 36
Tell Ashtara: 87
Tell el-Ash'ari: 89
Tell el-Husn: 89
Tell el-Oreinah: 74
Tel el-Samarat: 139
Tell er-Rameh: 94
Tell Hum: 58
Temple: 18,98-99,100,104,120, 142-153; *photos* 11,109,110,142-153
Temple Mount: 96,100, 101,102,113,116,117,131, 142-153; *photos* 49,99,101-103, 106-107,111,146, 148-149,150-151,153,182
Temptations:
 "Christ Tempted: 48-49
 Wilderness of: 44-47
Theodotian Stone: 104
Theodosius: 57,156
Theodosius II, Emperor: 116

189

Threx: 136
Tiberius, city:
 23,28,57,75,83,84
Tiberius, Lake of: see "Sea of Galilee"
Titus: 25,29,86,104,160,164,167
Tobiads: 94
Tombs:
 Eusebius of Cremona: 17
 Eustochia: 17
 Jerome: 17
 Joseph: 50; *photo* 53
 Lazarus: 131-134
 Paula: 17
Tombs, Jerusalem:
 Absalom: 101,159; *photo* 159
 Beni Hazir: *photos* 110,159
 David: 100,116,156
 Herod's family: *photo* 174
 James: 159; *photo* 159
 Jason: 101
 Jehoshaphat: 101
 Kings: *photos* 114-115
 Nicanor: 101
 Simon the Temple Builder: 101

Zechariah: 159; *photo* 159
See also "Where Is Golgotha?"
Transfiguration: 86
Transjordan: 37,86-94
Triple Gate: *photo* 149
Tulul Abu el-Alayiq: see "Jericho"
Tyre: 86,93
Tyropoeon Valley:
 96,98,102,104,129,
 142,147,163
Umm Qeis: 90
Upper City: 100,102,104; *photo* 150-151
Upper Room: 116,152,155-156; *photos* 109, 155,156
Valley of Jehoshaphat: see "Kidron Valley"
Varus: 94
Vespasian: 29,136,181
Via Dolorosa: 117
Wadi Kelt: 46,135,138,140,141
Wailing Wall: see "Western Wall"
Warning Stone: 149; *photo* 149
Warren's Arch: 149

Well:
 David's, Bethlehem: 13
 Jacob's: 32,50-51
 Woman at Sychar: 49
Western Hill: see "Mishneh"
Western Wall: 99,149
Wilderness:
 of Jesus' Temptation: 43,44-47; *photos* 44-45,46-47
 of John's Baptizing: 39-43; *photos* 39,70
 of Judea: 37,157; *photos* 37,70
Wilson's Arch: 102,149
Wisdom: 136
Xystos: 99-100
Yarmuk River,
 Yarmukian: 75,90
Yizreel: see "Jezreel"
Zacchaeus: 136,140; *photo* 136
Zealots: 27
Zeno, Emperor: 55
Zeus: 55,100
Zion, Mount: 101,116,157
Zippori: see "Sepphoris"

ABOUT THE EDITOR

William H. Stephens is design editor in the Sunday School Department of the Sunday School Board, SBC. Since 1974 he has been editor of the *Biblical Illustrator*. Dr. Stephens is a graduate of Grand Canyon College (B.A.), Southwestern Baptist Theological Seminary (M.Div.) and the The Southern Baptist Theological Seminary (D.Min.). He has edited a number of periodicals, served as a book editor for Broadman Press, compiled and contributed to a number of books, and is the author of *The Mantle* (*Elijah* in paperback).